DANCEPLAY

DANCEPLAY

Creative Movement
for Very Young Children

DIANE LYNCH-FRASER

Illustrations by Joyce C. Weston

Authors Choice Press
San Jose New York Lincoln Shanghai

Danceplay

Authors Choice Press
an imprint of iUniverse.com, Inc.

For information address:
iUniverse.com, Inc.
620 North 48th Street, Suite 201
Lincoln, NE 68504-3467
www.iuniverse.com

Originally published by Walker Publishing

ISBN: 0-595-12701-0
Printed in the United States of America

NOTE: Until someone invents a satisfactory genderless singular pronoun, unsatisfactory substitutes must suffice. The author has chosen to use the traditional "he" and "him," but emphasizes that this in no way reflects anything but usage, which she has been unable to improve upon, while recognizing the need for improvement.

Contents

Foreword

"Postural muscles are the hiding place for the emotions. Inhibition of movement limits kinesthetic awareness and perception, which are essential to psychological awareness . . ."

Charles Darwin
Expressions of Emotion in Man and Animals

Although we may receive tension from the environment, we do not store it "out there," we store it in our bodies. Without the opportunity to release this tension we become locked in certain postures and their corresponding attitudes. Our emotional repetoire becomes confined and hence, our aspiration to create ceases. We cease to feel the complete span of our emotions. What we want to achieve in our lifetime, however, is a harmony of mind and body so that the intellectual, the emotional, and the physical will work together towards a healthy balanced individual.

No single individual has advocated the significance of physical creativity in the first six years of life more than Maria Montessori, the Italian educator and psychologist. During this period the child has acquired an overwhelming amount of knowledge which will prepare him for the rest of his life. Before Montessori, educators believed the age of formal learning began at six. With the methods they employed they were correct in assuming this, as these could only be effective after the child had reached the age of reason. They had neglected to note that somehow the child had already assimilated a wealth of material, which he could never again duplicate before he entered elementary school. He had acquired a mass of coordination skills, a pattern of cultural and social adjustments, and all the nuances of a highly sophisticated language. The reason for the child's easy adaptation and learning, according to Montessori, is that our conscious and subconscious states have then not separated. We experience the world totally and do not yet possess a governing superego restricting what we can or cannot do. Our minds are open and all-absorbing. We have still what Montessori termed an absorbent mind. Modern society, in its quest for an antiseptic environment, has greatly neglected the child's inherent need for creative physical experiences.

Montessori felt that the body harbored a tremendous creative power that had escaped intellectual man. Contemporary educators and psychologists have erroneously assumed movement to be separate from higher functions. One thought of exercises as something to keep "fit" or "healthy". They had grossly underestimated the role of the body as a direct link to the brain.

It is only through expressive movement (call it "dance" in its essence) that higher life expresses itself completely because it employs both mind and body. It is precisely here that we venture onto the rich territory of non-verbal communication. We do not experience another human being purely on a verbal basis. Our concept of a person is a sum total of sensation, ninety percent of which is physically communicated.

As far as intellectual functioning is concerned, we have generally associated schooling with sitting motionless at a desk for long stretches of time. But mental functioning is connected with bodily expression and dependent upon it. If this necessary cycle is broken, a child's senses will suffer and he will remain on a lower level of mental and sensory functioning.

Man is a fantastic creature. His vast imagination and ability to express himself have helped him to accomplish the very feats which separate him from all other life forms. Man starts out as the weakest and most entirely dependent animal and yet grows through his creative capacity to better the environment, to ease mental and physical pain, and to create an abundance of aesthetic wealth. Only man has ideas.

Once society realizes that the education of small children is rooted in redirecting their physically creative capacities, the whole concept of movement will take on a new precedence. We must address the entire person, not just his mind. It is only then we can achieve the pure harmony of the human psyche that all cultures have heralded since time's beginning.

Liljan Espenak, M.A., D.T.R.
Director of Creative Therapies
New York Medical College

Introduction

"Thus goeth the body through history, a becomer and a fighter. And the spirit—what is it to the body? Its fights' and victories' herald, its companion and echo. Elevated is then your body, and raised up; with its delight, enraptureth the spirit; so that it becometh creator, and valuer, and lover, and everything's benefactor."

Frederick Nietzsche

Children are curious. They want to learn. As any parent of a toddler, including myself, can attest, young children are continually exploring—more accurately, perhaps, disrupting the environment. Their physical energy appears insatiable. Yet this is the way they learn about their world.

DancePlay harnesses this energy, directs it, and allows the parent and child to experience the learning process together—and have fun at the same time. These exercises are based on seven years of experience working with children of all ages, backgrounds, and mental developments. It has been my observation, and that of other educators, that one cannot isolate a child's physical development from his intellectual and social life. This is not to say that if Johnnie cuts his teeth late, he will be a social misfit. However, a child given the impetus to explore himself and his environment in what seems to be a purely physical sense will be more free to communicate and accept intellectual and social concepts. Parents and teachers in this country are becoming aware of this integration. Effective communication and interaction are the rudiments of education.

Following this introduction is a chart of normal developmental sequences that will allow you to gauge your child's performance. It is divided into four aspects: physical, sensory-motor, emotional, and social. Remember, the ages at which specific processes occur are approximate. Do not become anxious over seemingly delayed activity. Development can never be precisely measured.

The activities are divided into three levels of difficulty, and range from the more tangible to the more abstract. The same exercises may occur in each level with additional variations. The exercises need not be done in any special order though their presentation has been logically arranged. Preceding each level is an introduction for your convenience. Here you will find a description of what the following exercises are trying to achieve in all areas of your child's development.

There are a few requirements for all of the exercises. You will need a phonograph or a tape machine for the suggested music. The records or tapes can either be borrowed from the library or purchased from your local discount record store. Several exercises will require you to either prepare materials such as cut-outs or drawings or have certain props available, such as a wind-up toy or a piece of ribbon. If your floors are uncarpeted, you will need a soft thick blanket or a mat upon which to do some of the exercises.

Always have yourself and your child attired in comfortable clothing. Set aside a special time to be together. It need not be an extended period. Your child's attention span, especially if he is under three, is extremely short. Thirty minutes should be the maximum time allotted to any group of activities.

Begin slowly. Exercises will need to be repeated often until both you and your child are comfortable. He will also prefer certain exercises and demand their repetition.

Be patient and allow him to respond. Remember, there is no failure here. Children learn from imitation. Practice the exercises yourself. The more you do them, the more you will understand them. This will help you to alleviate any problems your child may have.

Do not expect your child to have the same interpretation you do. He may surprise you with a few delightful renditions of his own. Let him teach you. The more creative you allow him to be, the more accepted he will feel and the more encouraged he will be to continue.

The next point I want to make is that your child is an individual. There are certain exercises he may be reluctant to do, not because he is intellectually unprepared but simply because he isn't interested in the subject matter. Now, my first suggestion in this situation would be to check your presentation. Find out how you can make the material more interesting to him. If this doesn't work, it may be that this particular exercise does not appeal to him. That is OK. It is nobody's fault. Do not pressure him into anything he really doesn't want to do. This may alienate him; and you may then have difficulty presenting other exercises that could interest him more if he had not acquired a negative association with the previous one. Another suggestion may be to wait a while, go on to different exercises, and then present the previous exercise in a new context.

You will also encounter the situation in which your child will insist on the repetition of an exercise to your own utter boredom and exhaustion. You will be completely drained and there your child will be, dragging you by the hand, insisting on another "round." If this happens, try to incorporate a more relaxing exercise towards the end, one that may quiet him down. If this doesn't work, be calm and reassuring, let your child know your feelings. Work out some kind of compromise—that you will continue later or that you will do something equally enjoyable as a substitute or better—your spouse or an older sibling will take over!

Although these exercises are specifically geared toward children from eighteen months to four years old, there is no reason older siblings and friends cannot benefit by them. Get your teenage babysitter involved! If you have a number of children in the family, include them. Older children like to be given responsibility, and what a wonderful way to create warm family interrelationships! Again, if you do include older children, don't create rivalry by kindling a competitive atmosphere. Make sure you demonstrate that whatever anyone has to contribute is of value in some way.

The exercises are presented in developmental order. Level I deals with the tangible, Level II brings the tangible into the abstract realm, and Level III culminates all of this information dealing with both abstraction and the creative imagination. Your child handles his world in much the same way. He first notices that an object is a ball, then that the ball is round and red, and finally that he is a performer in a circus juggling this ball.

Now realistically, though there might be an exceptional 18-month-old child who could comprehend the material presented in Level III, these exercises are ideally presented when the child is between 2½ and 4. His language skills are more developed then and will enable him to participate more fully in these particular exercises. This is not to suggest that no part of Level III be presented to a child under 2½ years but that you gradually build toward these exercises, progressing first through Levels I and II. If the earlier exercises present no difficulty then I see no reason not to advance to the material included in Level III. If your child is older, perhaps three, I feel it is still important to include exercises from Levels I and II to begin. Your child will undoubtedly pass through these exercises more rapidly than the 18 month old. Levels I and II are the foundation for later material.

Whatever material you choose to present, I always suggest a warm-up. This warm-up may include the limbering exercises from level I or any other stretching exercises you and your child can devise. The warm-up prepares the body to move and gives your child the time to adjust to the idea that this is your "special time" together.

Lastly, enjoy yourself. Parents are people, too. You need to relax your parental responsibilities for a while and concentrate on your fringe benefits. The time from 18 months to

4 years old is so exciting. Never again will you be able to recapture with such fascination the emerging personality of your child. Take advantage of this time and share. Help your child discover the wonders of himself.

Developmental Chart

I am including a developmental chart for several important reasons, yet I wish to emphasize one thing very strongly. No matter how complete and studiously researched a chart may be, it can never be more than a guide—a kind of road map that offers you a number of alternatives to a given destination. I feel the need to stress this because western society has become so competitive, especially with our children, that we have lost sight of the true meaning of the term "development." Development is growth, expansion, evolvement. These processes are gradual. They are transitional processes that require assimilation and conversion, the ability to absorb information and use it to teach yourself. This does not happen overnight and certainly not in the 30-minute span of time you may spend doing these exercises with your child. Your child is not in a contest with anyone. It may take a number of repetitions before he can understand a certain concept. Be patient. Just because he doesn't seem to be giving adequate feedback the first time certainly doesn't mean he is not ready for your material. He is approaching these exercises in the same way he might approach a warm bath—sticking his toe in first and then taking the plunge.

Lastly, there are some sexual differences in development that I have not included in the chart itself but which I would like to mention here. The reason I choose to include this information is so that when you present these exercises, you understand that there is more involved here than just your child's developmental age. By the time a child is 2½, or possibly even sooner, he will recognize his sexual identity (whether he is a boy or a girl) and this recognition will bring a new response to the exercises. Your child may decide that a particular movement is or is not done by a member of his sex. This reaction can of course be met by the parent of his sex demonstrating the movement and establishing that while sexual differences do exist, in most ways boys and girls are very alike. Physically, a toddler boy will tend to be slightly taller and heavier than the toddler girl of a corresponding age. This situation will reverse itself as they approach adolescence when the girl will mature more quickly. Girls develop language and are toilet trainable earlier. Boys are more active— they may run or climb more than girls do. Now there are many theories as to why this is so. Some say it is hormonal, others environmental or cultural. I feel both of these factors play a part. No matter what the U.S. Constitution says about the equality of the sexes, boys are still encouraged to be more aggressive and competitive than their female counterparts, girls are encouraged to be more social and articulate. Culture cannot be changed overnight. The tendency prevails.

The chart is organized into four categories of growth: a) physical b) sensorymotor c) emotional, and d) social. The physical aspect includes just what is happening to the body—how it is growing and just what physical systems are available to the small child. The sensorymotor aspects are the physical abilities a child acquires when relating to his environment. He takes in information through his *senses* and makes the appropriate *motor* or physical response. The emotional aspect includes basically how the toddler feels about himself and the world around him. The social aspect is how your child chooses to adjust himself in society. Society, at this point, means his family.

These categories are further divided with respect to age. First from age 18 months through 2½ years, then from 2½ years through 4 years. Now, this is not to say that there are not many variables contained in each of these periods. A 22-month-old is certainly different from a 29-month-old, yet their likenesses correspond enough to be included in the same age grouping. These categories are set up simply for convenience, not as absolutes.

Developmental Chart

Ages 18 months (1½ years) — 30 months (2½ years)

PHYSICAL
Average Height: 2 feet 10 inches (34 inches)
Average Weight: 26 pounds
Child is about half his/her adult height.
Child is about 17% of his/her adult weight.
Appetite will begin to decrease.
Meats and fruits are the most important foods while the essentiality of milk and other dairy products lessens.
He generally eats one complete meal per day consisting of a protein (meat or fish), a green vegetable, a fruit, a complete carbohydrate (whole grain bread), and one 8 oz. glass of milk. Other smaller meals may include an egg, another piece of fruit, some cereal, half of a sandwich, and two 8-oz. glasses of milk.
Sleeps an average of 12 hours per night and takes one nap of approximately 1–3 hours per day.
Has 1–2 bowel movements per day, generally after a meal.
Urination occurs more frequently than bowel movements, about 2–5 times per day.
Deciduous or primary teeth that have appeared so far include: 2 lower central incisors, 4 upper central incisors, 2 lower lateral incisors, 4 first year molars, 4 canine teeth, 4 second year molars.

SENSORYMOTOR
Stands and walks alone.
Walks carrying heavy objects.
Holds onto objects while climbing.
Goes up staircase one step at a time.

Runs with certainty.
Holds things with certainty.
Takes long walks.
Kicks ball.
Says "no."
Names objects in pictures.
Pulls toys behind him.
Begins to move things with a purpose.
Begins imitative activities.
Likes to perform simple household chores—clean and dust.
Responds readily to music with bodily movement.
Can identify body parts.
Climbs with support.
Starts using toothbrush.
Begins to dress oneself.
Uses cup and spoon at mealtime.
Makes sentences of three words.
Builds a tower with several blocks.
Knows name.
Turns pages in book.
Can jump.
Uses blunted scissors.
Girl may be toilet trainable (bowel and bladder control).
Can draw a line.
Has a vocabulary of about 200 words.

EMOTIONAL
Begins having temper tantrums.
Becomes very stubborn.
Needs to be read to.
Likes bath.
Likes to smash and mess food, paint, clay.
Begins to have favorite toys and objects, such as a blanket.
Needs discipline, must learn to avoid dangerous actions.
Begins to use words as substitutes for action. For example, he
    may approach a stove, say "hot" and withdraw hand.
Has a great need to explore the environment.
Acquires phobias about everyday events—e.g., may be afraid

he will be swallowed up by the bathtub drain or eaten by the vacuum cleaner.

Can be very aggressive.

Develops a fear of the dark.

Begins to note sexual differences.

Objects become "mine."

Will want to know where babies come from.

Begins to use the terms "I" and "you."

Has a morbid fear of body damage or mutilation—may be very upset about a cut finger.

May refuse to eat because he is preoccupied with his activity.

Is able to accept imaginary substitutions for desired things. For example, if he can't have a bear, he will become a bear himself, or play with his teddy bear.

Develops negativism, has difficulty blocking own wishes— e.g., can't keep his hands out of your cosmetic case no matter how many times you say "no."

The postponement of an urge requires great exertion.

Becomes extremely willful.

Begins to whine.

Has very "real" nightmares.

SOCIAL

Begins to love his parents deeply and tenderly.

Begins to love himself.

The love of his parents becomes so strong that he may, on occasion, even diminish his own wishes to please them.

Can identify usual company—knows names of parents, siblings, close friends, and babysitters. Is uncomfortable, initially, with strangers.

Wants to do good so that he can like himself.

May strike other children and siblings, even parents, in defiance if they interfere with his wishes.

Begins to acquire imaginary friends. These friends come to personify his failings. They, not him, are responsible for his "indiscretions." This personification also helps the small child "do battle." It is easier to fight something outside of yourself than inside.

DEVELOPMENTAL CHART/15

If there is a new baby, there will be jealousy, no matter how
well prepared he is for the new arrival.
Becomes afraid of parental anger, especially if it is accom-
panied by "booming" voices.

Ages 30 months (2½ years) — 4 years

PHYSICAL

Average Height: 3 feet 3 inches (39 inches)
Average Weight: 36 pounds
Child is about 61% of his/her adult height.
Child is about 27% of his/her adult weight.
Has established definite food preferences.
Typical diet may include: 1/3 cup juice, ½ cup stewed or fresh
fruit, ½ cup cereal, 4 oz. meat, 1 baked potato, 2-3 slices
bread or toast, 3 teaspoons butter, and 2-4 8-oz. glasses
of milk.
Sleep is still about 12 hours per night though napping time
may begin to taper off.
Bowel and bladder control (toilet training) should be accom-
plished by his third birthday though there may be
"accidents" well into the fourth year.
Child has all his baby teeth—twenty in all.

SENSORYMOTOR

Can dress and wash himself quite adequately.
Combs hair.
Able to feed himself and prepare very simple foods, e.g., pours
cereal into a bowl, breaks carrots or lettuce into pieces
for salad, pours juice from a pitcher into a glass.
Dresses and undresses dolls.
Puts simple puzzles together.
Draws circles and crosses.
Attempts to draw himself and other objects in the environ-
ment, though unsuccessfully.
Begins to understand abstract concepts.
May stammer slightly.

Aids in household chores, e.g., taking out the garbage, open-
ing the mailbox.
Rides tricycle.
Can balance on one foot for a few seconds.
Can tell a short story.
Begins to count and learn the alphabet.
May begin to read aloud.
Can identify three colors.
Has a vocabulary of several thousand words.
Likes music, will sing favorite songs or lullabies.

EMOTIONAL
Adopts the "help-me-to-do-it-myself" attitude.
Likes to play "house."
Begins to understand the concept of cause and effect—that
everything is not "magical."
Asks the questions "what" and "why."
Begins to develop a conscience.
May believe he is omnipotent, adopt an "I can do anything"
attitude or a "you have to do as I say" attitude.
Develops highly exaggerated stories—learns to lie to avoid
avoid punishment.
At times, it may seem that nothing matters but his own feel-
ings. However, as he approaches four years, he will slowly
begin to move away from his totally egocentric world but
will occasionally indulge in an "I am God" routine.
Begins to feel guilty when he enlists parental disapproval.
May engage in seemingly cruel acts—crushing an insect un-
derfoot and then inspecting the results with a morbid
pleasure.
Needs to be told the truth, e.g., especially about difficult
situations, death in the family, etc.
The power of the imagination begins to take over and thrive
and is an aid in overcoming fears and understanding the
feelings of others (the child has to *imagine* another's
feelings).
Wants to know more explicitly where he came from—needs

clear information about the sex act, though not more information than he asks for.

May frequently assume the procreation process corresponds to the digestive and elimination processes.

May develop guilty feelings—if he says a "bad" thing it may actually come true.

SOCIAL

Gives names and attributes qualities to toys (dolls especially).

Plays with peers.

Needs nursery school or a structured social playgroup.

Needs increased periods of separation from parents.

Develops a roster of accusations for "friends," e.g., "Mary spits," "Johnny stole my toy."

May resort to namecalling and outlandish threats, e.g., "I am going to kill you dead" (which are best ignored).

By investing in his self-love, he slowly begins to transfer these feelings to others and form friendships.

Slowly begins to appreciate the feelings of other people.

May inspect the genitals of his friends, especially those of the opposite sex.

Needs to see the toilet processes of the opposite sex—this is usually provided in nursery school.

May develop Oedipal tendencies, e.g., "When I grow up, I am going to marry Mommy."

May begin a rivalry period with the parent of the same sex.

Slowly begins to identify with the parent of the same sex in an initial effort to gain the attention of the parent of the opposite sex. This represents the beginning of role modeling.

The child begins to curtail the handling of his genitals in public. He will, however, continue to do so in private.

Begins to introduce others into his wishes, e.g., "I want to take Mommy, Daddy, and Susie to the merry-go-round."

Level 1

Introduction to Level I

I start with the basics—slowly limbering the body to respond. The exercises in Level I are designed for all age groups. Children from 18 months through 2½ will, of course, find these exercises more challenging than a three- or a four-year-old. However, even a four-year-old needs the muscular limbering and strengthening aspects gained from these exercises. The stretching exercises (1–4) are special. They promote flexibility, relaxation, and concentration. They also demand eye-to-eye contact. This commands attention. And they involve a great deal of touching. Children need tactile sensation to be able to understand. All of what we learn must be felt through the tactile organs before they enter the brain. Simply, children like and need to be touched in order to learn. Children who are deprived of early tactile experiences later on show little or no interest in the environment upon which they will depend for their development.

Touching relieves fear, makes a child confident. When he is confident, his surroundings become attractive, inviting. He is in motion, with the urge to discover. A frightened child will be repelled by those very things that could prove exciting. He will cling relentlessly to his mother—always terrified that he will be left alone.

All of my exercises are rich in what I like to term "Touching Repertoire." The child is touching himself, touching you—absorbing these experiences. He is learning through imitation. His eyes, his fingers, his entire body have become his teachers.

I concentrate on the spine, the back. Everything, every sensation begins here. Releasing tension and increasing flexibility in the spine produces the same effect in the personality. The central nervous system, of which the spinal column is a part, is responsible for the perfection of our thought. It is our motivating source. Motion is an integral part of our total development. The muscular system must be used to support the intellectual and spiritual or emotional parts of our lives if we are to function at an optimum capacity. One cannot, must not, isolate the energy of motion from the energy of thought. If we do so, and man only uses those muscles absolutely necessary to a particular type of physical work, then his mind will remain at the same level. The mind, in a sense, will become detached from the body. With this detachment, the mind can no longer direct the body. However, through using these exercises, you can start your child on a lifelong project of developing his physical abilities and thereby enhancing his mental development.

The spinal exercises are designed to incorporate the abdomen and the extremities. The abdominal muscles are the only support we have for both the lower back and the extremities. Strength in this area is essential for satisfactory locomotor activity. Without it, walking, running, jumping would be at best, clumsy, if serviceable at all. The foot exercises are also mandatory because it is the feet alone that are responsible for the balance of the entire body.

The later exercises in Level I begin to foster the imitation process. Imitation is more than mere mimicking. Many mammals can be taught to perform complex patterns of movement but that is hardly comparable to the human learning process. Children must first develop the ability to imitate. They do this by slowly mastering their muscles. It is only by refining these motor activities that they become "coordinated." Coordination is the process by which several different groups of muscles come together to accomplish a set goal.

The use of music, which will be further elaborated in Levels II and III, is vital to the development of verbal skills. While speech is a conscious process, music is an unconscious process. Yet both these skills emanate from the same center in the brain. Music and dancing together are our most personal expressions of ourselves. The small child who has not fully assimilated his conscious state can respond to music without monitoring himself the way an adult will. He does not know good music from bad and he doesn't care. While language tends to separate people, music will unite us. It is universally understood.

The small child experiences his own inner rhythm and hammers it out with his feet or claps his hands. He yearns to communicate this exhilarating experience to those around him. As in primitive culture, the child experiences the joy of sound before he experiences the joy of language. A man alone playing on a drum is satisfied only so long. Then he needs an audience. A child exposed to music has a greater motivation to communicate with the world than one who is isolated. He will reach a point where his need to be closer to the rhythms of other people will inspire him to speak.

A child is attuned to his surroundings, almost instinctively. The objects he sees and feels play a greater part in his growth than are usually attributed to them. In the exercise that concludes Level I, we begin to touch the "tip of the iceberg." In this handling of objects both familiar and foreign, we can see the small child's ability to conceptualize and absorb. A child is never satisfied to merely *see* an object. He needs to stroke that beautiful piece of material (with his dirty hands). He *needs* to touch it. To restrict his explorations brings cries of rage. He smells it, tastes it, and lastly dances with it to demonstrate his own feeling about it. Now he understands it. He has absorbed it. A child must never be a spectator. He needs to be a participant. Only in action can a child learn.

Level I: The Exercises

1. "Good Morning"

OBJECTIVE: to limber the upper body, back, arms, and open chest cavity

MATERIALS NEEDED: soft thick blanket or exercise mat

DESCRIPTION: Start seated, "Indian style," facing your child on the floor. Hold his hands in yours. Open his arms to the side, extending them fully. Slowly, bring his arms together, folding them over his chest in a "bear hug."

Gently extend his arms over his head. Slowly, still holding both hands, stretch laterally to the right. Bring him back to the beginning seated position with both arms overhead. Now stretch to the left. Return to center. Lower the upper body until his head touches the floor. Return to the starting position and repeat three additional times.

2. "See My Feet"

OBJECTIVE: to limber the lower body and extremities, stretch hamstring muscles

MATERIALS NEEDED: soft thick blanket or exercise mat

DESCRIPTION: Have your child lying on a soft mat or blanket. Bend both his knees into his chest. Hold both of his ankles with your hands. Gently stretch his legs to their full extension, toes back. Return his legs to the beginning position. Repeat the exercise seven more times.

3. "See My Toes"

OBJECTIVE: to increase flexibility in the feet and ankles.
MATERIALS NEEDED: soft thick blanket or exercise mat
DESCRIPTION: Again your child begins lying on his mat or
blanket. Take his right leg by the ankle. Run your index
finger slowly over the sole of his foot, starting from the
heel. As you approach the toes, you will note them begin
to curl into an arch. This is a natural reflex. Now grasp
his toes with your hand. Reverse the process by gently
pulling his foot back into a flexed position. Repeat this
exercise seven more times. Now repeat the entire exercise with the left foot.

4. "Open and Close"

OBJECTIVE: to stretch the inner thigh, promote flexibility
in the hip socket, strengthen lower stomach muscles

MATERIALS NEEDED: soft thick blanket or exercise mat

DESCRIPTION: Child begins lying on his mat with his knees
bent into his chest. Hold his ankles with your hands.
Gently straighten his legs to their full extension. Slowly,
open both his legs into a "V" position. Now bring the
insides of his legs back together. Bend his knees back
into his chest. Repeat this exercise seven more times.

5. "I Sit Up/I Lie Down"

OBJECTIVE: to strengthen the stomach, arm muscles, and
the lower back

MATERIALS NEEDED: soft thick blanket or exercise mat

DESCRIPTION: Start facing your child while seated. Hold
both of his hands. Slowly lower him to the floor using
your hands as a support. Move your body slightly
forward to encourage this downward motion. When he
reaches the floor, grasp his hands more firmly and pull
him to a seated position, making sure that his chin is
down into his chest. Repeat this exercise seven more
times.

NOTE: As you do this exercise, you will note that your
child will begin to pull himself up off the floor to the
seated position while holding your hands. This should
be encouraged, because it teaches him to use his own
strength.

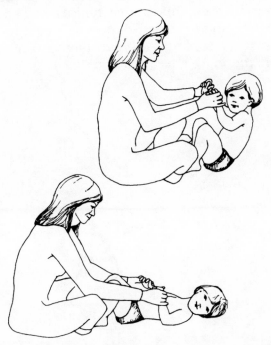

6. "My Rocking Chair"

OBJECTIVE: to relax the back, to reduce fear and inhibition

MATERIALS NEEDED: soft thick blanket or exercise mat

DESCRIPTION: Begin seated alongside your child's left side
on a soft mat. With him remaining in a seated position,
bring his knees into his chest. Grasp both his knees by
wrapping your left hand behind his right calf, your left
forearm pressed firmly against both his shins. Support
his back with your right hand at the base of his neck
between his shoulder blades. Make sure his chin is into
his chest. Slowly lower him to the mat. Now lift him to
the seated position. Repeat seven more times.

NOTE: After a few repetitions, your child may wish to do
this exercise independently. If so, remain alongside him.
Help him wrap both his arms around his knees in the
seated position. Get into the beginning position yourself. Wrap your arms around your knees and do the
exercise with your child. It may take a while for both you
and he to be able to return to the seated position without
assistance. The secret is to create momentum. The faster
you roll, the more energy you will have.

7. "The Top"

OBJECTIVE: to stretch the hips, the upper back, to increase balance and equilibrium, to establish breath control and relaxation

DESCRIPTION: Start facing your child, seated, with the soles of your feet together. Hold your ankles. Assist your child into the same position. Breathe in deeply through the nose. Fill your stomach with air. Sit with your spine erect, shoulders down, chest slightly forward. Show your child how your stomach expands "like a balloon." Have him feel your stomach. Now blow all the air out of your stomach through your mouth until your stomach is flat. Roll back slightly off your "sits bone," in order to pull your stomach in, then soften the back and drop your forehead down over your heels. Elbows are directly over the insides of the knees, helping to stretch the pelvis and the hip joints. Your child will be watching and examining you. Have him feel your spine, your chest. Tell him how the air goes in and out of his body. Repeat three more times from the beginning by yourself. You may have to repeat this several times for your child's satisfaction.

Now have him, with your assistance, try this himself. Beginning with the soles of the feet together, have him hold his ankles. Sit along his left side, your left hand along his abdomen, your right hand on his upper back. Have him breathe through his nose and fill his tummy with air (like a balloon). Have him look at his big round tummy. He may want to put his own hands on his stomach and explore. Using your hand against his stomach, have him blow all of the air out of his mouth and make his tummy soft. Gently lead him to lower his upper body so that his forehead is over his heels and have him "kiss his toes." Repeat three additional times.

Remain in the seated position with the soles of your feet together, holding your ankles. Sit erect, shoulders down, chest slightly forward. Shift your body weight to the right so that you fall onto your side. Your ankles are still being held. Roll onto your back so that only your lower spine is touching the floor. Keep your chin down into your chest. Now roll onto your left side. By reversing the shift in your body weight you should be able to return to the beginning seated posture. Parents as well as children will need to practice this one.

Your child will immediately want to imitate the "top." Have him begin in the previously described posture. Squat down in back of him. Grasp him firmly around the waist with both hands. Roll him onto his right side. Begin to roll him onto his back. As you do so, slide your hands upward under his arms. This is to keep as much of his upper body off the floor as possible. His chin should be into his chest. Roll him onto his left side and return him to the beginning seated posture. Your child will eventually be capable of doing this on his own and "spinning like a top."

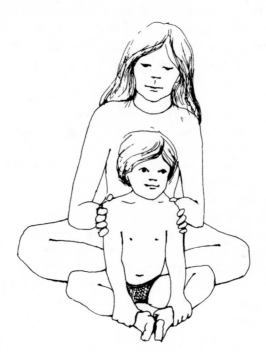

8. "The Shrimp"

OBJECTIVE: to promote spinal flexibility

DESCRIPTION: Have your child start either on a soft mat or on the floor lying on his back. Stretch his arms and legs long like a rubber band. Try to have his "tailbone" touch the floor. He does this by pressing his tummy flat. His knees may need to bend a little to accomplish this. Now very slowly help him bend his knees into his chest and curl his upper body down so that his elbows are bent across his chest and his head is almost touching his knees. Slowly, roll him onto his right side. Now open his arms and legs to their full extension while still on his right side and roll him onto his back once again. Perform the same procedure to the left side.

NOTE: This exercise should have a fluidity—a continuity, like a shrimp in motion under water. It may help to show your child pictures of live shrimp, since many children are unfamiliar with this animal in its natural state. The rolling and curling of the spine as well as the rolling and extension of the spine need to occur simultaneously for maximum benefit.

A simple variation would be to have your child curl his upper body first, then curl his lower body—again rolling to the right side. Now he uncurls his upper body before his lower body and rolls onto his back. This helps to clarify the distinction between the upper and lower body. This same exercise can be done in reverse. This time, the lower body may curl before the upper body.

9. "The Cat"

OBJECTIVE: to increase spinal flexibility, to stretch hamstrings

DESCRIPTION: Start on your hands and knees alongside
your child. Have him do the same. Tell him you are going
to make a table with your back. Make sure your spine is
perfectly straight, including the neck. Look at the floor.
Now arch your back, pressing your stomach down to the
floor and your buttocks to the "sky." Lift your head back
and look at the ceiling. Elbows are slightly bent. Pull your
stomach in now and reverse your spinal arch, dropping
your head down to look at your abdomen. Elbows are
straight. Repeat this exercise three times.

Your child may begin to imitate you before you
complete your demonstration. Touching and exploring
are strongly encouraged. Most children will try to speed
up the exercise so that it becomes a jerking motion. Help
your child to slow this down by placing one hand on his
lower abdomen and the other on his lower back. Take
him through the exercise "petting" him like a "little
kitty." This inspires the soothing effect required for this
exercise. Try to have him master about four repetitions.

Now tell him that when the "kitty" gets angry, he may
hunch his back to the "sky" or "way up." Still on your
hands and knees, flex your toes back underneath you
and press the balls of your feet into the floor. Straighten
your knees, press your hands into the floor and look at
your knees. Bend your knees and return to your beginning position. Help your child to do the same. Again
complete four repetitions.

10. "My Magic Body"

OBJECTIVE: to identify and gain awareness of body parts

MATERIALS NEEDED: recording of rhythmic music

DESCRIPTION: Sit facing your child with your legs crossed "American Indian" style. Have highly rhythmic music playing, preferably a song with which your child is familiar. You may sing or hum the song if it makes you and your child more comfortable. Begin to clap the rhythm of the music. Wait for your child to reciprocate. When you have his attention and interest in the music, start to pat your individual body parts calling them by name. Start with the more identifiable body parts such as the head, knees, feet, and toes—body parts with which your child is already familiar. Children like an immediate sense of accomplishment. When he begins to imitate you and has mastered this, go on to more challenging body parts, such as the elbows, ankles, and hips.

Your child may surprise you and initiate the selection of body parts himself. If he does, follow him. This activity will evolve to a point where both you and he are alternately taking initiative with the further selection of body parts.

Get your child's attention. Make eye-to-eye contact and begin to tap one of his body parts yourself. Always say the name of the body parts while you are tapping. Your child may allow you to tap him for some time. Children love to be touched. Take his hands and indicate that you want him to tap you. You may lead him to specific body parts, such as the head, to begin. Once he gets comfortable, allow him to choose. Whatever he touches, name it for him.

There is no set structure for this exercise. Sections of activity can be intermingled. You may tap yourself, then immediately choose to tap your child. Encourage him to respond in the same way.

11. "Hear the Music"

OBJECTIVE: to increase sensitivity to sound and heighten communication

MATERIALS NEEDED: a recording of a "march" and a "waltz"

DESCRIPTION: Have two styles of music prepared for this exercise: a slow-to-moderate march and a waltz. Start playing the march and moving in a traditional manner—lifting knees high, swinging arms. Wait for your child to respond. If he becomes confused, take his hand and slowly lead him into motion. He may choose to do something entirely different. Allow for this expression. You may follow him. Use this same procedure with the waltz music. The traditional movement pattern here involves a circling action with arms raised.

NOTE: No matter what action is chosen for the marching music, it will most likely be characterized by straight angular movements. In contrast, the waltz music provokes a round, smooth, flowing action.

12. "The Secret Box"

OBJECTIVE: to further foster the giving and taking of physical movement and the awareness of objects

MATERIALS NEEDED: old grocery carton filled with household items and toys

DESCRIPTION: Fill an old grocery carton with familiar objects, household items, and toys (e.g., scarves, tennis balls, plastic hoops, costume jewelry, old hats). Have some lively music playing. Your child can play this dance game with friends or the two of you can enjoy it alone. Choose any object with which you feel comfortable. Now begin to move freely with the object (e.g., swaying a scarf overhead or side to side; bouncing or rolling a ball). Keep your motion in time with the music. You may share your object with your child or encourage him to choose an object of his own with which he can move.

In the beginning he will be more comfortable to imitate your movements. Later you will see him initiate his own. If he does, follow him. Do not expect him to approach an object traditionally. He may want to jump up and down on a hat (make sure it is an old hat!) rather than put it on his head and skip around wearing it. Remember, creativity is the focal point. His suggestions can and will be more important than your own.

As you move, change tempos, move both slowly and quickly. Do not remain standing for the whole exercise. Literally, get down to his level. Feel free to crawl or roll on the floor. Try to explore movement with as many objects as you possibly can. Naturally, you and your child will have favorites or be more secure with some objects than with others. However, do take a chance. Be courageous!

Level II

Introduction to Level II

In Level I, you helped your child discover his body. In slow, carefully-planned exercises, you gently stretched and strengthened his spine, his abdomen, and his extremities. He began to learn about himself, his senses, and the environment in which he lives. If the central concept in Level I is discovery, the central concept in Level II is awareness. The exercises in level II are best presented when your child is approaching 2½ years. They will have to be presented very slowly at first, yet as your child approaches three, much of the material in Level II will have been absorbed, and he will be ready to begin Level III activities.

Your child has "found" his body and examined it. He needs to integrate what all of this means in a cognitive sense. The young child must first learn that he is in fact separate from his environment. He must learn at an extremely early age that there is a world that takes place outside of himself and a world that takes place within his own self.

Now you say, isn't this rather existential for a small child to comprehend? Well, yes and no. First, one of the milestones in child development is that a child learns to deal with separation anxiety. The small child must understand that when mommy goes out for an evening with daddy that they are not truly gone simply because he cannot see them. They are going to another place in which they will exist for a time in much the same way he exists in his own place, and then they will return. A small child will never accept your daily or evening excursions unless he can truly understand this.

There may be additional complications when your child realizes you are going somewhere that he would like to go. Now he is reluctant to stay with Aunt Susie. However, this is a different conflict. The child understands here that you do not simply vanish into thin air but do in fact go somewhere else. How does he learn this? Well, there are several theories and all of them depart from one another at some point. However, they all agree on two essential ideas: 1) the small child arrives at the realization of his own separateness through the sensations he feels in his body. 2) this concept is something that must be *learned*. It is not innate.

A toddler has to learn body awareness. He must develop something called "whole body schema." Of course, a toddler must have some sense of whole body coordination just to be able to walk and jump. However, it is interesting to note that though a very young child will be able to distinguish one finger or two fingers if you hold them up in front of his face, he cannot tell if you are touching him in the back with one or two fingers. If he falls down and cuts himself in a place he cannot see, or gets an insect bite on the back of the neck, he cannot often tell where it hurts, though he knows he is hurting somewhere. In other words, though he has some sense of whole body coordination, it is incomplete. The more specific and more structured a child's motor activity becomes, the more fully developed his body "schema" will be. There are studies that indicate the learned nature of body "schema." An example of this would be adults who, due to disease, infection, or accident have lost an extremity. These extremities are still "felt"; and hence we arrive at the term, "phantom limbs." The nerves for these extremities are still active though the limb is gone. On the other hand, children who are born without a limb never experience "phantoms," even if the nerve for this missing limb is still intact. The nerve must have been used for the limb to be felt. This suggests that body schema is only acquired with the proper stimulation.

Body schema is essential to our perception of ourselves and our personal identity. From a very early age we see ourselves as big or small, beautiful or ugly, weak or strong. We all know examples of extremely attractive successful adults who, because of how they perceived themselves as children, never come to appreciate their own beauty or intelligence. It is extremely important that the young child have a positive picture of his body—that his body is good, pleasing, and reliable. The only way he can confirm this initially is by your approval, encouragement, and his own positive body experience. All of this will play a part in his life goals, aspirations, and intimate relationships. Of course, body schema can never be complete or unflawed. Over a lifetime, we change our body image many times. This can be commendable especially when it is commensurate with a life change.

With the discussion of body parts comes the previously tabooed area of infantile sexuality. Some readers may be shocked to think that I could refer to an innocent toddler as a sexual being. However, we are sexual from the day we are born. Some theorists believe us to be sexual even "in utero." The important thing is that a child be satisfied with his own body and especially those parts that we deem sexual. This early satisfaction is preliminary to healthy sexual relationships in adult life. If a child's sexual parts are ignored or presented as naughty, he is certainly not going to feel good about himself. Of course, culture and individual modesty dictate your own feelings about your own body. Never do anything with which you feel uncomfortable. Many pediatricians encourage communal bathroom visits. This, of course, is up to your discretion. Whatever you do, your male child is certain to notice that piece of flesh between his legs and your daughter is going to notice that daddy makes "wee-wee" standing up. If mommy is pregnant, there is no way he is not going to notice her "fat" belly.

I will never forget the time I was doing the Magic Body exercise, Level II, with a group of ten toddlers. We all sat in our carefully arranged circle and each child was asked to volunteer a body part and then show us a little dance about that body part in which everyone could join. I turned to a particularly precocious little girl of about 2½ and asked, "Now, Pammie, which body part would you like to talk about?

Pammie responded, "Nipples," and promptly stood up rubbing her chest and stamping her feet in her own "nipple dance." Toddlers notice a great deal more than they have been given credit for.

The best thing to do is wait for your child to notice, then give him his answers. Our overly concerned society nowadays has produced a new kind of parent who is prone to giving too much rather than too little information. Listen to your child and give him the information he has asked for, not an excerpt from the *Journal of the American Academy of Obstetrics*. If you have questions, ask your pediatrician. He will know what information your child can accept.

The service these exercises perform as far as sexuality is concerned is that they can, if presented carefully and lovingly, provide your child with a healthy body image. This healthy image will spread into all of his life activities, making him confident and assertive about his body, his thoughts, and his feelings.

Here I also would like to discuss a rather distasteful subject, yet I feel it is essential when discussing body awareness as a total experience. The issue I am referring to is that of toilet training. Never has so much rhetoric been given to what may be the most unintellectual of topics. Any parent who has arisen from a reasonably restful night's sleep and stepped into a puddle of fresh "pee" certainly understands the term "frustration." What do you do? The only answer is wait. Somewhere, unless there is something fundamentally wrong, your child will toilet train himself between 18 months and three years. Girls will adapt sooner than boys. How soon your child chooses to do this, and more important how he feels about this experience is entirely up to you.

First, let's take a look at what is physically happening. In late infancy, the child learns that he has eliminated, then he learns that he is eliminating, finally he learns that he is about to eliminate. It is only when he has reached this final stage that you can begin to toilet train. All of the aforementioned processes require a sensitivity to inner motor activity. There is also a sense of timing and control here.

The process also requires a special kind of interaction between the parent and the child. Civilization, not nature, has introduced the toilet. Running, eating—these are natural processes, but defecating and urinating on a large porcelain throne certainly are not. Your child is only going to do this, initially, if he feels it will in some small way gratify you. He needs first to have established a warm loving relationship with you.

Although your child will never be toilet trained overnight (I am suspicious of any parent who claims this), through the body awareness exercises presented in Level II, your child will attain the bodily control that may be instrumental in achieving simple, unanxiety-ridden bowel and bladder control.

Around the same time a child learns about his body, he begins to understand the concept of responsibility. What, at two years old? Yes, at two years old. If you notice the behavior of a 22-month-old (for instance), when he falls down, he is more angry at the floor for coming up and hitting him on the head than at himself for darting recklessly over the kitchen floor. Now this is acceptable behavior for a 22-month-old child. Unfortunately, many adults continue to conduct the business of their lives in much the same manner. They consistently assign blame for their faults as well as their success to other people or environmental factors such as "luck" or the "supernatural." This can be a very frustrating, if not a totally debilitating, philosophy. Though we can never totally assign ourselves with absolute responsibility, we can help our small children to establish that vital, though inevitably blurred, boundary between self and the environment. We begin by examining our bodies.

As the small child learns the command of his individual body parts, he also learns that they can be explored and tested. He comes to know two very vital things about his body: 1) that he can experience certain pleasures in bodily movement. The actions, in and of themselves, are desirable. 2) These pleasurable actions can help him communicate further desires to the environment. If he cannot attain what he wants himself he can use his body to make these desires clear to another who is capable of fulfilling his wishes. His body, in a sense, becomes the link between his internal and his external wishes.

With this new desirable body awareness comes control and self-discipline. All of these terms, unfortunately, for some people have come to mean oppression and self-deprivation. It need not be that way at all. The small child first needs to be protected and secondly wants discipline. It is a kind of security for him. This control, surprisingly enough, cannot merely be exerted by you. It needs to come from within himself—from within his own body. You, as a responsible parent, can lead your child to experience this greater sense of self. With this bodily control comes a kind of pride—"I don't always need to have things done for me. I can do them myself and succeed."

Muscular coordination, of which I spoke briefly in Level I, is the result of this bodily control. Muscular coordination is peculiar in human beings. We are born with practically nothing. All of our motions must be shaped and coordinated.

How different it is for other animals. Almost from birth, they can walk, run, climb, even fly. Interesting too, is that man is born with no purpose for action. He is almost symbiotic at birth. He can't even protect himself. Abandonment can almost always result in death. Animals have highly developed instincts. They know what to do. Though we too have instincts, they are minuscule. Everything we do must be learned, sensed through the body before it can be assimilated.

It almost sounds as if we are at a great disadvantage, yet our ability to learn, to coordinate movement is unsurpassed. In a lifetime we can learn many highly diverse activities. Yet these movements come only with experience—education. The professional tennis player has the same physical anatomy you do, he just uses his differently and more often. As Maria Montessori, the renowned early childhood educator aptly said, "Every person is the author of his own skills." We learn through experience—experience in action.

Controlling and enhancing muscular coordination does more than merely strengthen muscles and aid in circulation, if both the mental and the physical concept are connected and occur simultaneously; it stimulates mental development. It is truly a miracle that man coming into the world with no special aptitudes or gifts (as do other animals: monkeys can climb, fish can swim, etc.), can master both his mind and his body to accomplish almost anything, provided he is given the proper stimulation. In a sense, he is freer than the animals because he can choose what he is to do. And that truly is his advantage—he can choose and master anything.

Touching is also extremely important. The small child cannot tell the characteristics of an object just by looking at it. He does not know whether it is hot or cold, soft or hard. A child must experience touching—the touching of objects. When he constantly has them snatched right out of his hands, he will destroy the thing he finally does get his hands on, because he doesn't know what to do with it. In Level II, the purpose of touching becomes more sophisticated. In Level I, touching is primary for security and reassurance. It inaugurates the learning process. In Level II, it is used more for communication—for a means of reaching out to the world. To a small child, mother or father *is* the world. He or she is the embodiment of all things desirable. Somewhere around two years of age, your child will begin to notice your preferences. You get angry when he goes near the stove, runs out into the street, plays with detergent. Touching, however, is the first way in which he understands your feelings. When he is naughty, you do not give him a big hug. If he has endangered himself, a sharp slap on the hand may be warranted. In most instances, however, a child should experience touching as pleasurable and rewarding.

If you have a strong loving relationship with your child, he will be eager to learn about and experience his world without taking dangerously uncalculated risks. The proper touching stimulation will teach him to enlarge his influences to include touching experiences with relatives and friends. Most children, thankfully, are not openly intimate with strangers. (Undue fear, however, is something to be discussed with your pediatrician.) A normal response to a stranger would be a meditative stare, perhaps followed by a "hello" or a wave of the hand. Do not expect your child to climb readily into the arms of anyone—even if it is your mother on her annual visit. Touching himself, followed by touching you, and then followed by the touching of intimate friends, is the normal sequence. This sequence can be encouraged during your intimate playtime with each other and also with his friends. Touching relieves undue anxiety and allows the child to pursue different relationships and goals in a healthy relaxed manner.

As his sense of touch increases, he will become extremely sensitive to his body. Around the age of two or three, your child will exhibit an unusual concern about cuts and scrapes, especially if there is blood. He has decided, at this point, that his body is a container. Blood can only mean a leak.

Basically, a child's sense of body wholeness or completeness radiates into the child's dealings with his world. If his perception of himself or his body is distorted, the likelihood of a distorted perception of the world is eminent.

The presentation of shape is our first attempt to deal with abstract versus concrete thinking. Both types of thinking are necessary to healthy mental and emotional development. Concrete thinking has to do with the present moment while abstract thinking deals with dimension—time, space, shape, etc. These perceptions, like everything else, must be learned. It is interesting to note here that the small child often associates the shape and functions of his body with the shape and functions of his environment. Trees and flowers seem to have arms but no legs. Scratches that he sees in the sand, or clouds overhead, seem to take on human appearance. This further demonstrates the essentiality of a healthy body image. Again, the way a child sees himself (his body) is the way a child sees the world.

Up until about 25 years ago, there had been little research done on the nature of children's thinking. The behaviorists had practically banished all inner processes, believing that all development was controlled by the environment. However, this reasoning is incomplete and thanks to the pioneering work of Jean Piaget, we now know a great deal about children's cognitive experiences. We also know that it differs quite a bit from adult reasoning.

Children's thinking is basically ego-centered. This is not to say that the child is selfish—just that he cannot see that others have their own perceptions and desires independent of his perceptions and desires. That is why small children are notorious for offering bits of their previously chewed food to parents and friends. It tastes good to him, why shouldn't you enjoy some?

With the learning of shapes the child begins to experience the highly abstract notion of dimension. Even though he will still continue for some time to pet the doggies and kiss the mommies in his storybooks, he will eventually learn that these are just mere representations. Shape has both two- and three-dimensional characteristics. This third dimension leads us to the concept of space. We can hardly discuss shape without including spatial concepts. The concept of shape and space are totally meshed, yet they are often confused by the exploring toddler.

For example, your toddler sees a piece of cardboard on the floor and exhausts himself trying to pick it up. He cannot see that he is standing on it! He cannot reach a glass on one side of the table. He does not think to go around the table to the other side, where he could easily retrieve it. He cannot interpret the relationship of quantity and space. If you spread several toys over your living room floor, he will automatically think there are more toys than if you place the toys right next to each other. When his fruit juice is poured into another glass, he deduces that the quantity of the liquid as well as the size and the shape of the glass has changed.

It is the integration of shape and spatial concepts with which he is having difficulty. The more opportunity a child is given to solve shape and space problems, the greater his chances of diffusing this information into his practical life. Of course, the complete thinking process takes a long time to develop. Even when your child is ready to leave home, you will question his thinking. The shape and space exercises in Level II are designed to provide a testing arena for abstract thought. There is nothing to win or lose here, with the exception of your approval. Slowly and comfortably you are guiding your child through his environment.

The learning of language, numbers, and the alphabet are all abstractions. These methods of communication are merely substitutes for thought. They were devised to represent something else. The science of shape and space is a mathematic of sorts. The knowledge of these abstract thoughts represents a clearly organized mind. Even those with the wildest of imaginations, if they are in fact successful, maintain an order in their thinking. Great music, literature, choreography, all need an order. Nature provides the small child with many experiences, yet rarely does she present him with the materials necessary for the learning of abstract thought. These materials must be cultivated by conscientious parents and teachers.

A child's need for order in relation to shape and space is one of his stronger motivating forces. Any distortion or change in the toddler's environment is almost immediately noted. The small child must learn not to fear these changes, but rather to adapt and be able to place new ideas in the order of his life.

Although the concept of time will not be learned by your child until long after toddlerhood, it is necessary to address this area from the point of learning and integrating abstraction. Let me give an example: Music is a time dimension—it exists in time. Art and sculpture are space dimensions—they exist in space. However, motion, movement, dance (whatever you may call it), embraces both these dimensions. It takes both time and space to create a dance. When a child is in motion, he is instantaneously absorbing both of these abstractions, though in an extremely fundamental way. At this point, I would like to relate a little story that I feel illustrates this discontinuity. One evening my husband, my daughter, and I were walking home from a nearby restaurant. Suddenly the sky opened and it began to pour. We had anticipated this event and were prepared with a small umbrella. The umbrella, however, proved to be very inadequate in a rainfall of such intensity. We were forced to huddle under a canopy of another restaurant until the rain tapered off. My daughter, 22 months old at the time, had not been in a downpour of this nature for a long time. She sat in my arms, trying to clarify this experience. She determined that it was a shower, that it was water, and that it was wet. I added a new word to her vocabulary, "rain." "Rain," she repeated. I was delighted. When the rain stopped, we resumed our walk home. Being an "astute" parent, I looked at my child and asked, "Where did the rain come from?", expecting her to point to the sky. Instead she pointed back to the restaurant canopy we were standing under. As far as she was concerned it had rained right where we were and nowhere else. Even though she saw the puddles and confirmed them as "wet" or "water," she did not assume that these puddles were the result of the same rain that had occurred just outside of the restaurant canopy. In fact, she didn't even care. The puddles were there—that was that. A toddler's handling of causality is very casual. They would make very poor attorneys. So the exercises in Level II provide another important service besides body awareness. They introduce the child to the nature of abstract thinking and the integration of abstract thoughts.

Level II also introduces another desirable quality, that of concentrated effort, and with that, self-motivation. In Level I, much of the work is being done by you. You are carrying out a great deal of manipulation. Even in activities free of your manipulation, your child is largely imitating your behavior. True, this requires concentration, but it is of a different nature. The kind of concentration required in Level II is that of an independent human being involved in his own thought and action and not solely the thoughts and actions of others. (This will be discussed more fully in Level III.) Your child is learning to draw on the material you present and incorporate it into his own activities.

Most educators and psychologists agree that to acquire concentration, a child needs materials—toys and games that hold his attention. If a child is to amble about meaninglessly, abnormalities are bound to develop. Simply put, a child's order of thinking and his order of movement are inherently bound to his developing concentrated effort or concentration. Again, concentration must be learned. If it has to be learned, then it must be taught. You must get involved with your child. He cannot learn without you. Given the most stimulating environment, a child cannot grow without your careful guidance.

This is another service these exercises provide. They provide the materials for guidance. A child's merely "being occupied" with something is different than his "concentrating in" or being "absorbed by" an activity. It is the latter process we are interested in enhancing, since this is the basis for intellectual development. Children who are merely given activities to keep them out of their parents' hair are going to approach their school work later on with the same ambivalence, or even with hostility.

Of course, parents and children need time away from each other. This is healthy. A child should be able to play alone for a time. Interesting is that the more constructive time you spend together, the more constructive time the child can play alone. He will learn to teach himself. Children should learn one thing—that "learning is fun."

The more of a child's personality that can be brought to an activity, the greater his level of concentration. Simply put, the more of a child's physical, emotional, and intellectual abilities that can be used during an exercise, the greater his interest. The child who is easily distracted, in a sense, is possessed by his environment. The child who develops concentration is only possessed by himself. Clearly concentration paves the way for perseverance. We all know fully grown people who haven't the vaguest idea of what they want. These are not stupid people. They just never learned the value of concentrated effort. A child who is given freedom within a concentrated structured environment is always at a greater advantage than one who is either given no attention at all or one who is smothered so that he distrusts his own decisions.

Again, I wish to emphasize the importance of allowing

your child to make choices within an exercise, even to initiate the exercise himself once he has had it presented to him. The sensitivity of a parent is indicated by his knowing when to advise and when merely to observe. This is particularly difficult and even frustrating for some parents. They themselves are in as much need of attention from their child as the child is in need of attention from them. They say they want their child to be average, but in fact they want their child to be superior. This is not wrong—all parents want gifted children. But children need to be freed from their parents' absolute control. As difficult as it may be to accept, the more capable your child becomes, the less he will need you. This, however, can give you a new perspective. Your child's love becomes more unconditional. He loves you because you are you, and not simply because of what you can do for him. You also will have a little more time for yourself.

One more word. Do be patient with your child. Allow him more success than failure. Remember, these exercises are not a "one-shot deal." They were developed to be presented again and again as an ongoing process. There is a saying that "perfectionism breeds chaos." This can definitely apply here. You want your child to enjoy these special times together. Make them as pleasant and yet as challenging as they can be.

Level II: The Exercises

1. "My Magic Body"

OBJECTIVE: to identify the functions and interactions of body parts

MATERIALS NEEDED: a recording of rhythmic music

DESCRIPTION: This exercise is essentially a continuation of "My Magic Body," Level I, exercise #10. Once you have established with your child that he does have very special body parts, it is important for him to know what these parts can do. I recommend beginning in much the same way as you did for "My Magic Body," Level I. Sit facing each other in "American Indian" style. Have some familiar music playing. (Music, at this point, is for background, just to make the two of you more comfortable.)

Ask the child about the different parts of his body (e.g., Where are your hands? your elbows? etc.). See how much he knows and have him find these body parts first on himself and then on you. This game can go on for a few minutes.

Now make good steady eye contact with him and say you would really like him to take a good look at his toes. If you haven't already, take off your shoes and socks. Look at your toes, then look at his. Ask him where *his* toes are. Where are *your* toes? Ask him how many toes he has and count them for him. Have him do the same. Now tell him that toes are so much fun because they can do so many things. Fan your toes apart as wide as possible. Tell him your toes can open just like a flower. Take his toes and spread them with your fingers. Then have him try to fan his toes himself.

Now curl your toes tightly against each other as if you were making a ball with your foot. Help him to squeeze his toes. Now combine these activities by alternating the squeezing and the fanning of the toes. Tell him that his toes can also wiggle—wiggle all around. Go ahead, wiggle those toes.

Progress to the feet. The toes are part of his feet. The toes help his feet to do many things. The feet are even more fun than the toes because the feet can do more than the toes can do by themselves. Point your foot into an arch and then flex your foot all the way backward.

Again manipulate his feet in much the same way and then have him repeat the sequence by himself.

If your home environment permits or if you have kind neighbors, tell him that you can also stomp very loudly with your feet. Begin to stomp or march vigorously about the room. Children love this and may be reluctant to stop this activity. When you feel he has had enough, tell him that his feet can also be very quiet. Rise up onto the balls of your feet and tiptoe. Tiptoeing is something you do when someone is sleeping and you don't want them to wake up. Again, alternate the activity. Tell him that feet can either be loud and stomping or quiet and tiptoeing.

Have him examine the "bumpy bones" just above his and your feet, called ankles. The ankles are special "locks." They hold your feet onto your legs. The ankles can help your feet make circles. Begin to rotate one of your ankles in a circular motion and have him do the same. You may do this in either a standing or a seated position.

Progress through the entire body is this manner—the basic formula being: first, to identify the body part, second, to establish how this body part moves, and third, to find out how this body part is connected to the rest of the body. Of course, there are some body parts that will have a lesser range of motion than others. For instance, the knees can straighten and bend but they could never have the versatility of the hands and fingers. Other body parts cannot move at all, (e.g., the ears). This concept should be explained to your child. Some body parts have a special kind of work to do. They need to be able to move in a special way. Other body parts have work that does not require them to move so much.

It is also important to address more than just the extremities. Children and parents alike tend to see their body only in terms of hands and feet. Remember that you have a back, which you can arch and curve and tilt from side to side, a stomach and chest cavity that you can expand and contract by utilizing your breath control, even buttock muscles that can be squeezed tightly together. Make sure you explore all of these possibilities. You will undoubtedly discover new things about your own body. If the body part is located in the rear of the body, like the spine or buttocks, turn your back. It is important that your child be allowed to examine you fully while you are demonstrating. This is the only way he can become aware of exactly what these body parts are capable of doing.

It is also helpful to make the appropriate analogies. For instance, your leg can move like the swing in the park—back and forth. Your back can move the way a kitty's does when it gets angry. These analogies will help illustrate how these body parts function—how one part of the body moves in relationship to the rest of the body.

To conclude, take your child over to the mirror. Have him take a good look at his face. Start by examining the face as a whole. What can the face do? You can make an angry face, a happy face, a surprised face, or a very silly face. You can make your face very small. Squeeze the parts of your face together—close your eyes and tighten your lips. Now make your face very big. Open your eyes and your mouth very widely. This is very exciting to small children. Tell your child to make the silliest face he can and then you try to copy it.

When he has mastered this, examine the individual parts of the face—the eyes, the nose, the mouth. There will be parts of his face that are difficult to move, like the nose. There are also parts he will not be able to move at all, like the ears.

You may not be able to complete this exercise first time around. Chances are you and your child will be exhausted before all of your body part alternatives have been considered. Do not be concerned. Each time you do this exercise, add new body parts. Try to explore even the obscure body parts like the tongue or the rib cage. The more body parts your child comes to identify, the more he will want to know about.

2. "The Wiggle Dance"

OBJECTIVE: to understand the concept of motion versus stillness to help your child understand the concept of bodily control

MATERIALS NEEDED: a recording of some rhythmic music

DESCRIPTION: Have some highly rhythmic music playing. Again, make it something your child enjoys hearing and with which he is familiar. Tell him you want him to do the "wiggle dance" with you. Begin to wiggle and shake your body all over. Have him do the same. Make sure you are involving as many body parts as possible—the head, the legs, the hips. Try to keep in time to the music. When you are both actively in motion, ask him to stop his head from wiggle dancing but keep the rest of his body in motion. Granted, this is not the simplest action to coordinate, but it does come with practice.

Slowly begin to eliminate certain body parts from the "dance," e.g., legs stop wiggle dancing, hips stop wiggle dancing, etc., until the entire body is still. Now reverse the process. Tell your child to allow his fingers to wiggle dance, his feet to wiggle dance, etc. Finally, his whole body will be alive with wiggle dancing. This "dance" can be completed and then reversed several times. It takes a great deal of concentration and coordination for both you and your child. However, it can be mastered with a great deal of fun in the process.

3. "How do you do it?"

OBJECTIVE: to further explore the use of body parts in our everyday environment

DESCRIPTION: Sit down with your child and have a little discussion. Talk to him about the various things he does or has seen you do during the day. He may kick a ball or open a door. He may see you climb the stairs or clear a table. Now, what body parts does he think help to do these things? In reality, it is the integration of many body parts that are engaged in an activity; however, it is important for him to know that his body was not designed arbitrarily. Certain body parts do certain things.

Take the example of kicking a ball. How does he kick the ball? What body parts does he use? Tell him to show you how he does this. If he is confused, you can use a ball to demonstrate. Have him show you what he does with his leg even when he only pretends to use the ball.

Explore several activities together. Get down on the floor and clean up that "spilled milk," or "juice." Maybe take a pretend laundry to the washroom or fix a pretend pipe under the sink. After a number of repetitions he should understand that it takes a number of body parts to accomplish even a simple task. Remember to exaggerate all these activities for your child's benefit.

4. "The Touch Game"

OBJECTIVE: to further awareness of body parts

DESCRIPTION: Once your child has fully explored all his available body parts, he is ready for this exercise. Tell him you want to play the "touch game" with him. Start simply and directly. Tell him to touch one of his hands to one of his knees. Now touch his elbow to his knee. Touch his hand to his hip. Continue in this manner, using the more familiar body parts first and following with the more obscure. Try to incorporate as many body parts as possible.

Now introduce yourself into this game. Tell him to touch one of his hands to one of your knees. Touch his head to your stomach. When two people are involved in this game, more body parts can be explored—simply by virtue of their greater accessibility. No one can touch his toe to his shoulder (except perhaps a very fine gymnast or ballet dancer), but his touching his toe to *your* shoulder is simple—a great deal of fun. Try to find as

many unusual combinations as you can. For instance, a knee touching an ear, an elbow touching a big toe. Simultaneous touching of identical body parts is also fun—two heads or two buttocks bumping together. Explore all of the positions you can. Try to maintain these peculiar postures while moving about. Can you lie down and still have an elbow touching a hip? How about sitting or standing? Can you walk around the room while his hand is on your knee?

The possibilities in this exercise are endless. You can play this game often and still find new and exciting combinations.

5. "The Body Chain"

OBJECTIVE: to further awareness of body parts; to foster interaction and cooperation

DESCRIPTION: You will need a pile of little people in your living room or backyard for this one. Essentially, you are striving for the same goals here that you were in The Touch Game. The difference here is that aside from merely understanding the workings of his own body, you want to motivate him and his friends to *communicate with each other* in purely physical terms.

If the other children are unfamiliar with the game, which they most likely will be, divide them into partners, and demonstrate yourself with your child. When all seem to comprehend, you can begin to call out directions. "Everyone touch his partner's foot with his own hand." This will take some time to coordinate. It would be best not to have more than six children on hand. Small children do not take directions very well; however, if you yourself are participating, they will be ready to imitate you. Small children love to imitate and are quite good at it.

The next part of the exercise can be done in several ways. I prefer to line the children up seated on the floor. Tell them you are going to build a chain with their bodies (show them a chain if you have one handy). Address the child seated farthest to your left (or right) first. Tell him to touch his hand to "Mary's" knee (the child seated adjacent to him). When the two children have accomplished this, congratulate them. Now tell them that the body parts are stuck together like glue—they can't come apart until you say a magic word (invent a magic word or phrase like "break the chain"). Now "Mary" and "John" are hitched hand and knee together with this magic glue. Tell Mary that without moving her knee away from John's hand, she is going to touch her elbow to Susie's hip. There should be a good deal of giggling at this point as the children try to coordinate these awkward postures. Encourage them to keep their positions as long as possible. If they find this to be difficult, do not pressure them. Remember, this is a game as well as a learning experience. When you have completed this chain, call the "magic word," break the chain, and send them tumbling to the floor. You can now reverse the chain, if you wish, starting with the child who was previously in the last position.

Another way to approach this is to scatter the children slightly but still keeping them in close proximity. The directions will have to be more specific, however, and you will have to tell each child whom he is to touch, since there may be several children in his vicinity. The interest in performing this activity in this manner is that it creates a more sculptural effect when completed and also enables the last child in the chain to hook onto someone else.

6. "Round and Straight"

OBJECTIVE: to introduce your child to the concept of shape

MATERIALS NEEDED: a selection of both round and straight shapes

DESCRIPTION: You may have to do a scavenger hunt before you begin this one. Look around your house for a number of small objects that are decidedly either round or straight (e.g., tennis balls, rulers, plastic bowls, and pencils are all suitable) If you are particularly industrious, you may search through old magazines or catalogs, then cut and paste the pictures of round and straight objects that you found on colorful pieces of construction paper.

Sit down with your child and see what he knows about different shapes. See if he can identify whether the objects you have selected or the pictures you have found are either round or straight. Explain to him that there are basically two kinds of shapes: round shapes and straight shapes. Balls and balloons are very round. Tell him that you are going to make a round ball-like shape with your body. The simplest way to do this is to get down on the floor and curl yourself up into a fetal position. Have your child do the same. Ask him what a round ball can do. Can he roll or bounce like a ball? Can he move his round ball-like shape in any other ways? Experiment with different ways to move.

There are also straight shapes like the pencil and the ruler. Show him how you can make a straight shape with your body. Stand tall like a soldier with your arms at your sides. Have him imitate this shape. Ask him how he can move his straight pencil shape. A straight pencil shape can spin in a circle, it can tilt from side to side. You can lie down on the floor in your straight pencil shape and roll like a log. Again experiment with different ways to move.

When you feel your child has understood the distinction between round and straight, you may want to try this. Make a shape with your body (either round or straight, it doesn't matter). Now ask your child whether he thinks you are making a round or a straight shape. Reverse this process by his making the shape and your guessing what the shape is.

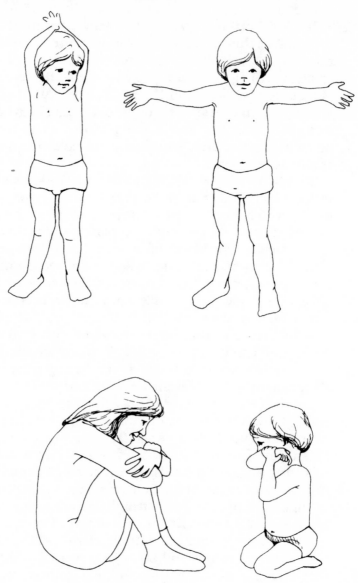

7. "Spaces"

OBJECTIVE: to introduce spatial concepts to your child

DESCRIPTION: You may choose to do this exercise either indoors or out. I like to at least begin this exercise outside
because there are more reference points available. When
you are walking outside with your child one day, casually
mention that the world is divided into many spaces.
There is a space for the air, a space for the ground, and a
space in which people work and play. The air space is
very high. The ground space is very low. There is a middle
space that is in between these two spaces. Ask him
which space he thinks he is in now. In which space does
he think the birds fly or the insects crawl? There are three
spaces: the high space, the middle space, and the low
space.

When you come indoors, sit down with your child and
discuss what kinds of activities you can do in the
different spaces. How about the low or ground space?
You can roll and crawl, do somersaults, slide on your
belly. How about the middle space? You can walk on
your knees, walk as if you are sneaking about with your
knees slightly bent.

NOTE: I don't encourage standing fully upright in the
middle space, simply because that would leave us very
little activity to do in the high space. Obviously, we
cannot take off like a bird. We must confine our activity
somewhat and use our imagination. Most children will
readily accept this concept. They too have come to
realize, with the exception of a few (the real adventurers),
that they cannot fly.

When you come to discussing the high space, try
tiptoeing with your arms reaching overhead—jumping,
leaping. Again, as with previous exercises, experiment,
try to find newer, more exciting ways, to move in the
three spaces.

8. "Shapes and Spaces"

OBJECTIVE: to foster the concept of shape and spatial integration

DESCRIPTION: After you have explored exercises 6 and 7 satisfactorily, your child will be ready for this exercise. Before you begin, discuss with him briefly the concepts explored in exercises 6 and 7. Tell him you want to put the shape game and the space game together. Does he think he could make a round ball shape in the low ground space? Show him how you can do this and have him imitate. Can he make a straight shape in the high space, or a round shape in the middle space? Remember to use your entire body when making a shape. This is essential if your child is to distinguish one shape or space from another. For example, when you are making a straight shape in the high space, get up on tiptoe with your knees and your back perfectly straight and your arms extended overhead. For a round shape in the high space, soften the body slightly and curve the arms as if you were holding a large round bowl overhead. If you want to make a round shape in the middle space, bend the knees slightly and round the back while curving your arms.

NOTE: A general rule of thumb: If there is a question as to whether a particular shape is either round or straight, look at the spine. If it is not perfectly straight, then it cannot be a straight shape. The same rule applies to round shapes. The entire body must work together to create either a round or a straight shape.

9. "I am a Piece of Clay"

OBJECTIVE: to further the awareness of shape, to encourage cooperative effort, to introduce the concept of passive versus active

DESCRIPTION: Before you begin this exercise, gather some pictures of sculpture. You can find these in newspapers and magazines. Have also a small piece of clay on hand. Sit down with your child and explain to him about sculpture. Tell him what a sculpture is and how it is made. A sculpture is made by someone called an artist or a sculptor. The sculptor looks around and when he sees something he likes (perhaps a tree), he takes a piece of clay, like the one you have, and "makes a tree" with the clay. Make a tree with your clay. Your child will want to try this himself. Give him the clay and have him make the tree (or whatever). Tell him that there are many other things the sculptor may like to make—dogs, houses, etc. Make a few of these things also. Sculptors also make sculptures of designs they keep "in their heads." Shapes that are pleasing to them but are not necessarily anything in particular. Show him some pictures of abstract modern sculpture. Make a few of these with your clay and have him reciprocate.

Now tell your child that he is going to be your piece of clay and you are going to be the sculptor. You are going to think of something you would like to make and then create it with his body in the same way a sculptor would make a sculpture with a piece of clay.

Have your child lie on the floor. Pat him and roll him, as he has seen you do with the clay. Now tell him you are going to make the shape of a tree with his body. Encourage him to remain passive during this exercise, allowing you to mold him into your desired shape. When you have completed one shape, try another. Make sure you include shapes in all spaces: high, middle, and low; and both kinds of shapes: round and straight. When your child is comfortable doing this and you feel he understands, you may reverse roles. You are the piece of clay and he is the sculptor. You, as well, should try to remain passive as the piece of clay—after all, it is his

creation! The only suggestion I would make is again to make sure he includes both round and straight shapes and high, middle, and low spaces.

This exercise becomes more interesting when there are more than two participants. If your child has friends over, present the idea of playing "sculpture." If the parents are present, encourage them to participate. Explain the concept of sculpture in the manner you did with your child. The best way to begin is to take the role of soulptor yourself and let everyone else be a piece of clay. Have the children scatter but still remain in close proximity to one another. They should each be on the floor curled up in a ball-like formation—like a piece of clay.

Go to the first child and gently "mold" him into your desired shape. Tell him that he must hold this shape like a statue until you tell him otherwise. Go to the next child and place him in a shape adjacent to the child you have previously molded. The second "piece of clay" should be touching the first child in some way. You are now using several bodies to make one sculpture. Proceed in this manner from one child to the next, always connecting the child to some previously molded body in the sculpture. By the time you finish, or perhaps before, all the children will be giggling as they find difficulty in holding their assigned shapes. Instead of allowing them to collapse upon each other, gently tap each one of them one at a time, lightly on the head and let them melt down into the floor like a candle and slowly roll back to their original places.

All children will want to take the sculptor's role now. Select one to begin and, of course, promise the others a chance. You may elect to be a piece of clay yourself or just monitor the proceedings. I generally opt for the second choice, as small children need direction and encouragement, especially when they are attempting something for the first time.

10. "Pick a Shape"

OBJECTIVE: to present the idea that the shape of an object in the environment can correspond to a shape you make with your body

DESCRIPTION: Sit down on the floor with your child and ask him to look around the room. What kinds of shapes are there in the room? What kind of shape is the table? What kind of shape is the lamp, the mirror, etc.? Pick an object from the room, the table, for instance, and tell him that you are going to make a straight table shape with your body. Make your shape. Now ask your child if there is any special shape he likes. Maybe he likes the plant or the vase on the mantelpiece. What kind of shape is that and how can he make it with his body? Absolute accuracy in shape is not too important here as long as your child is able to integrate the concept that shapes in the environment can correspond to the shapes he is making with his body. Of course, if he is trying to depict a decidedly angular shape and does so by curling into a ball, then he must be corrected. This game can go on indefinitely, as there are so many different objects that can be discussed and made into bodily shapes. Again, be sure to remind him and yourself about the two different shapes and the three different spaces. It is easy to become trapped on the floor, or low space, and not venture into new areas.

When you both have become comfortable doing this exercise, you might try this. Tell your child that you are going to put a certain shape into your body but you are not going to tell him what it is. He will have to guess. Be very deliberate in what you choose now, for you do not want to discourage him by choosing an obscure shape that he will not be able to guess. When he guesses, tell him it is his turn now. He will not be able to demonstrate as effectively as you were able to so ask him to help you. If you are really "stumped," ask him to tell you his secret.

11. "The Maze"

OBJECTIVE: to further spatial awareness

MATERIALS NEEDED: roll of masking tape

DESCRIPTION: Go to the hardware store and buy yourself a roll of wide masking tape. Go into your game room, kitchen, bedroom, whatever uncarpeted floor space you have. If you care a great deal about the condition of your floor, you may want to lay down a large sheet of white shelfing paper and tape it to the floor at the corners. Take your masking tape and begin to tape a maze or pathway made up of rectangular shapes to the floor (or shelving paper). Try to create as many enclosed spaces as possible.

You may have your child contribute to this design or you may present it to him as a surprise after you have finished. Tell him this is a special picture called a maze. A maze is a place with many special spaces and your maze is special because you have made it yourself.

Let's see if we can tiptoe on the maze. Begin to walk tiptoe on all of the pieces of tape you have laid down. Be careful to walk on all of the pieces. What else can you do with the maze? Let's see if we can make a different shape in every space in the maze. Go through the maze and make either a round or a straight shape in all of the maze spaces. Let's see if we can do different things in each space. You can spin in one space, sit down in another. You can jump up and down or hop on one foot. See how many activities you can devise.

12. "ABC"

OBJECTIVE: to introduce the alphabet, to further awareness of shape and spatial concepts

MATERIALS NEEDED: alphabet picture books, crayons, magic markers, construction paper

DESCRIPTION: If you haven't discussed the "ABC's" with your preschooler yet, this is the time. Gather all of your resources. Go to the library and take out some alphabet books. Get out your crayons, magic markers, paste, and construction paper. Make some colorful flash cards. Sit down with your child and ask him what he knows about the alphabet. The alphabet is made up of letters and letters make words. Words are in all of the books you read in him. Words tell stories.

Do not discuss too many letters to begin with. I suggest using O, V, I, and S—letters that are simple to create with the body. If his name or the name of one of his friends or siblings begins with this letter, bring it to his attention. It will make it more interesting for him. Start simply. Show him a picture or a flash card with the letter "O." Can he make this with his body? Can he make this "O" shape in the high space, the middle space, or the low space? Though it is not entirely necessary, it is desirable that he try to use his entire body. He may choose to shape the letter only with his hands in the beginning. This is perfectly acceptable, as long as the letter is suggested by at least one body part.

Once you have explored the letters that are less complicated, you may go on to the more intricate letters. Present these letters in the same pattern as before: introduce the letter with visual aids and make the shape with your body. It is a good idea to show your child the entire alphabet at this point—suggest to him that the alphabet does in fact have a special order (he may already know this, especially if he's been to nursery school). The alphabet starts with the letter "A" and ends with the letter "Z." Start with the first three letters, "ABC," and make them with your body. Do not attempt to get through the whole alphabet in one sitting. It requires far too much concentration for a small child. I would suggest maybe 5 or 6 letters to begin. Plan to present the others at another time. Again, always try to incorporate references into the activity. For example, "H" is the letter with which the word "house" begins, or "M" is the letter "milk" begins with.

13. "The Magic Yarn"

OBJECTIVE: to further explore shape and spatial concepts
MATERIALS NEEDED: strands of yarn
DESCRIPTION: Gather all of that yarn you have left over from well-intentioned sweaters, separate it, and cut it into armlength strands. Sit down on the carpet with your child and the yarn. Tell your child that this is magic yarn. You and he are going to make magic shapes on the floor with the yarn. When you have made a magic shape, you are going to try to make the same magic shape with your body.

Take a piece of yarn and give one to your child. Tell your child that you are going to make a special shape with your yarn on the floor. It is going to be a shape you have thought about yourself and that no one else knows about. Make your shape with your yarn and then put your body into that shape. Have him do the same.

Take turns at this for a while. Then have one make the yarn shape and the other put that shape into his body. Again, remember to use all shapes and all spaces.

14. "Bridges and Tunnels"

OBJECTIVE: to further explore spatial concepts, to introduce
    the concept of over and under

DESCRIPTION: Again, have visual aids prepared. Page
    through your old magazines for pictures of bridges and
    tunnels. You can also draw these yourself, if you wish.
    Tell your child that bridges and tunnels were made so

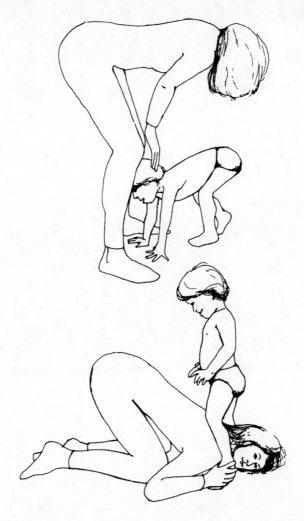

that people can go from one place to another. Bridges are built so that people can go *over* water. Tunnels are made so that people can go *under* mountains or water.

Do you think you could make a bridge or a tunnel with your body? Tell your child you are going to make a bridge. When you have made your bridge, encourage the child to "climb over the bridge." Now make a tunnel with your body. Tell your child to go through or under the tunnel. Now it is his turn to make the bridge or the tunnel. You will go over or under them this time.

15. "Boxes, Boxes"

OBJECTIVE: to further explore spatial concepts, to introduce
    the concept of inside and outside
MATERIALS NEEDED: grocery cartons
DESCRIPTION: Save several of your grocery cartons for this
    exercise. Have them of different sizes and shapes. Try to
    have at least one of these boxes large enough to hold your
    child's small body. Tell him that you want to make some
    special shapes with these boxes. Use your body in the
    two different shapes and the three different spaces and
    incorporate one of the boxes into a sculpture with your
    body. Give one of the boxes to your child or have him
    choose a box for himself. Have him also make a shape
    with his box.

    Now pick up one of the boxes and tell him that the box
    has two special places: an inside place and an outside
    place. You can make a shape outside the box or inside
    the box.

    Let's make a shape with a box and keep our bodies
    outside. Now let's make a shape with maybe one body
    part inside the box. Make another shape with your head
    inside the box. The grand finale—make a shape with
    your whole body inside the box.

Level III

Introduction to Level III

Level III builds on all the concepts presented in Levels I and II. These exercises are the most abstract—the most sophisticated. Your child's power to create is being developed here. He is being asked to draw on all the material presented thus far. The narrative stories introduced here present opportunities for integrating several different abilities. In these exercises, there is rarely one focus. Music, shape, space, color, and verbal skills may be needed to explore a single exercise. Level III exercises are best presented as your child approaches three years of age. At this point his language development is sufficient to allow for the understanding of the narrative stories presented in Level III.

You will note Level III exercises are comparatively less structured than Levels I and II. You are not being told exactly what movements to do. The realm of personal expression is important here. Your child is not merely isolating a given skill. He is being taught to balance this skill along with other aptitudes much in the same way that we do in life. He is not just walking. He is walking through a park, observing, taking in information, selecting a swing on which to play, and relating to others. He is becoming a person.

Level III allows for your child's greatest movement potential. You may ask why expanded movement is so important. There are many reasons. As a parent, you have emerged with your child from the relatively secure world of infanthood, in which your expensive lamps could remain on display in the living room, to the "battleground" of "toddlerhood" in which you are in constant anxiety over even your least-prized possessions. You can't even keep an old magazine lying around. Your child climbs out of his crib in the morning equipped only with his pajamas and a love-worn stuffed animal, and can turn your household upside down in a matter of moments.

Somewhere, around the age of three, things may begin to calm down a bit, simply because he has learned to avoid certain unacceptable activities. But his curiosity and need for motion have not ceased. For every unacceptable activity, you must provide an acceptable one. And it must be one that holds his attention equally. Children learn to enjoy constructive adventures as well as they enjoy their previously destructive acts. It doesn't take any more energy to do something constructive than it does something destructive. So why not encourage the former? Motion is vital to children of any age. To discourage or punish it is to disturb your child's inner workings. Expanded motion is a child's way of moving forward from the unconscious world of the infant toward the conscious thinking world of the adult, of which he will eventually be a part. Before a child makes any movement, he must absorb and store information in his unconscious. When he moves or dances, he is bringing visibility to his personality. The more rich these movements are, the more learning can take place. In the manner we condone thinking, we need to condone liberal moving.

Of course, as in everything, these activities need to be carefully guided, not in the context of restricting movement but in the context of enlarging it. Even if a child is not truly ready for the emotional or intellectual concept that you are presenting, the mere guiding of his body through the act will send messages back to his brain that will help him to understand. In a sense, you are waking up his brain, his feelings, through using the "push buttons" of his body.

I want to emphasize that here in Level III, which represents the synthesis of all of the information gathered through the activities in Levels I and II, the concept of movement as an embracing integrating force is of vital importance. Motion is not and cannot be an isolated event. Yet the nature of movement in childhood has often been misunderstood. Our school systems, until recently, have designated "exercise" as a lower function. Perhaps if exercise is considered only in terms of volleyball and other competitive games, it is. But a small child's body is more than that. It is the instrument of his emotions, his intellect, and his spiritual self. The body gives thought its expression. And what are thoughts without expression? The body is possibly the only unselfish entity we possess. Thoughts and feelings are self-contained. But the body brings these thoughts to the world—enables us to communicate.

I could continue my glorification of the higher functions of the human body "ad infinitum." However, the point I want to make is this: When you are presenting these exercises to your child, you are doing more than just playing a game, especially at Level III. You are enriching his cognitive and emotional life in far greater ways than you suppose. There will be times when you will present an exercise and presumably have no concrete response. Three or four days later, your child will come back to you with countless details about the event—some of which you won't even remember yourself. A young child, like an adult, sometimes needs time for things to sink in.

The focus of Level III is "integration." I have used this word countless times in the two previous explanatory sections, but without clearly defining it. Integration is the ability to perceive a situation as a complete experience. This ability can never be perfected—not even over a lifetime. However, it can be tuned and polished so that our life experiences have a greater clarity. Let me give a few examples. In the abstract sense, integration is like a cake recipe. If you eat all of the ingredients separately—the eggs, the flour, the butter, and the sugar, it wouldn't taste like a cake. In other words, for something to be perceived exactly as it is, all of the ingredients must be blended together.

How does this apply in practical life? We live in a multi-dimensional environment. If your child cannot understand all of these dimensions simultaneously, he cannot maneuver himself well within this environment. For example, your child understands the concept of shape. He sees that the world around him is not just one shape but many shapes that differ from one another. He understands that these certain shapes are not part of his body but part of his environment. This knowledge has come to him through sensations he has felt in his body numerous times. However, if he has not integrated the concept of space along with the concept of shape, he will not be able to judge how far away these objects in his environment are. Fortunately, abstract thoughts do tend to occur together, though the learning process can be a long arduous one.

Integration also involves the carry-over of intellectual thought into our emotional and spiritual lives and vice versa. This can be even more complicated because here we begin to venture into the area of subjective versus objective thinking. For example, a man has a lung condition. His doctor has told him that he should not smoke. Intellectually, he is not at a loss. He knows emphatically what he must do—he must not smoke. Yet he continues, for emotional reasons, to smoke. This action represents a failure of integration—not simply the failure of his intellect or emotions. Separately, this man's intellect and emotions may work remarkably well.

There are countless examples of integration failures that occur daily. Your child knows that he should not play in the bathroom. You have told him dozens of times. Yet he still goes in there, turns on the faucet, leaves it running, and is very likely to cause a nice flood on the bathroom floor. When you do catch him "red-handed," you are likely to find him reprimanding himself saying, "No, no. Mustn't do," just as he turns on the faucet. My daughter would stand directly before an engaging object she knew she couldn't have and slap her own hand in the manner of her Dominican babysitter, saying, "Pow-Pow," which loosely translates from the Spanish to mean "spanking." The small child does know his limits, yet he has not mastered his control system as yet.

The exercises in Level III present material which begins the learning of integrative processes, due to the wealth of experience from which a child is required to draw. With the understanding and utilization of integrative concepts come the development of morality, or perhaps a more accurate word would be "conscience." Conscience, in the traditional sense of the word, is a standard of action a person arrives at without the aid of outside systems to support it.

I am taking "poetic license" here, for my use of the word "conscience" does not merely include the realms of good and bad. I use it to include all subjective decision-making processes. For example, a woman comes home one evening from work. She has purchased a lamp. She has spoken to her husband about this purchase and has indicated that it was important to her. Her husband comes home and sees the lamp. He does not like it. He would have chosen something else. He does not choose to tell his wife this because he knows that this would upset her. Instead he tells her that her purchase is satisfactory to him.

Now there are arguments on both sides for this action. Some will say, yes, he did the right thing. What is the purchase of a lamp in the course of life anyhow? Others will argue, no, that was not the right way to handle this. If he didn't like the lamp, he should have said so. The truth is always the best choice. The integrative processes were involved here when the man made the decision not to tell his wife his true feelings. He decided emotionally that he did not like the lamp. Intellectually, he decided that not liking the lamp was the truth. However, he chose not to tell his wife the truth in order to protect his wife's feelings (and perhaps his own, in that he has had a hard day at work and doesn't want to start his evening arguing over a lamp). There was feedback between his emotions and his intellect, yet the choice arrived at is not indisputable. The decision being made here is not as simple as looking at a ball and deciding it is round, red, and exactly three feet away from you.

There are two kinds of conscience-related processes your child must learn: 1) those things he must do or must not do, and 2) those things with which he has a choice. The hard fact is that a two-year-old does not have a conscience and won't have one until nearly his fifth or sixth year. So why am I bothering to discuss it? Because a conscience is something that needs to be built, slowly and carefully over a period of time, so that when he reaches five or six, he has a sturdy structure of a conscience and not a tottering shack. The methods of parental guidance used in a child's earliest years are representative of the patterns of self-guidance or self-discipline that a child will demonstrate in his later life. If a child's only understanding of discipline has been a spanking or ridicule, once he outgrows spanking and parental ridicule and becomes an adult, he feels he can do anything he wants— good or bad, without guilt and for that matter, without pleasure. The child must learn from a very early age the full ramifications of his actions, so as to be able to make sound, rewarding decisions.

What these exercises provide, in a very rudimentary fashion, is activity that requires both structure and choice. The child learns, unconsciously at first, what he can or cannot do and what he can choose to do. All of this, of course, is done within your loving supervision. The toddler parent, in a true sense, is the child's conscience. Most psychologists agree that the toddler's urges are usually too strong to control and that redirection of these impulses is the best way to avoid the inevitable parent/toddler contest. The best way to keep your child out of the bathroom and the garbage is to engage him in an exercise that involves his entire personality. In short, an effective conscience functions very much like an effective parent.

Since the development of conscience is an internal process, it requires that the child develop something of his own to master it. Most children develop language. My feeling, and the feeling of many educators and psychologists, is that music is inherently bound up in the development of language. There is no known culture that has developed without music, and there is evidence that music came before language and, in a sense, set the precedent for language's existence. As I said in my introduction, and as many others have said before me, music is the universal language. It is the unconscious process through which the conscious process, language, emerges. Now, you ask, why should a small child be required to learn note values? For the same reason he is taught his "ABC's." These images represent the basis of our culture. As language is simpler to learn when one is young, so are musical theories. At 2½ years, a child does not know he is learning the alphabet or music theory, he is just playing a game. If you wait until he is ten years old and then demand he learn to speak French and play the clarinet, his response will be quite different. If he has not developed a warm relationship with language and music early in his life, he will probably just resent these demands. The development of language and musical skills are in direct correlation to the development of conscience and other control systems.

Now music offers another experience just as essential as developing conscience. It offers your child the opportunity to create. It has a catalytic quality. We all know the feeling when we have put in a particularly draining day at work and are duly fatigued. We switch on the radio tuned to our favorite station and suddenly we feel refreshed. The music has given us energy. The old "whistle while you work" theory is at play here. We are able to get more work done with less fatigue. Any industrial psychologist can tell you the value of music in the workplace. It increases production.

It is for this reason that I include music in most of my exercises. It is the motivating force that increases production. The production of what? Creativity. Which brings us to the question: Are we all naturally creative? Is creativity essential? I would like to think that we are all creative to some extent and yes, I feel creativity is essential. To be creative is to be able to devise new ways of doing the same thing. Life would be awfully dull without that.

We tend to think of creativity as something to be explored solely within the artistic realm. I feel this is an injustice. Creativity enters all of our lives. There are creative accountants, policemen, autoworkers, and waitresses. They do the same job that everyone else does, but they send out an energy that makes their lives and the lives of everyone around them more exciting and different.

As children, we start out with a kind of creativity more accurately described as curiosity. We need to explore things, to experiment with them, and understand them. We don't follow too much direction at this point—everything is new and exciting. We develop an imagination. This imagination is responsible for man's being able to see beyond what is already there. It is imagination that creates growth in adults as well as children.

The importance of imagination in child psychology cannot be overstated. Yet the child's power to imagine has often been relegated to fairy tales and nonsense stories. If a child can imagine illusion, then he can also imagine the truth. The exercises in Level III are asking your child to indulge in fantasy, but not in the traditional sense. He is being asked to go beyond the information given and venture into the unknown. The unknown he finds are the truths of culture— the seasons, wild animals, modes of transportation. Many of these things he may not have experienced as yet. He may never have seen a real elephant or flown in a real airplane. But through using the incredible power of his body and his imagination, he comes to know these things. In order for man to be considered intelligent he needs to master two mental powers: 1) that of abstract thinking, the ability to accept the existence of intangible concepts such as time and space, which can be measured (see Level II), and 2) that of imagination, the ability to create new thoughts and/or solutions about or for given information. Both of these processes are equally necessary to healthy mental functioning. In given individuals, one process is likely to prevail over the other, yet there must be a reasonable balance. When one nurtures purely the abstractive functions, the result is an extremely precise person who would not dream of investigating beyond what is already known. On the other hand, if one concentrates solely on the imaginative processes, he will have few skills to apply in his practical life. In other words, you want your child to understand the realities of his world but not be afraid to challenge them if the issue presents itself.

The manner in which the exercises in Level III are presented promotes both of these cognitive functions. Your child is not being asked to create snow in the springtime (though this is not a counterproductive concept), for that is not a cultural reality. Yet he is, within a winter context, being asked to surmise and explore the various snowflake designs—something that is purely from his imagination. The fault with some education (and that is changing) is that it considers the imitative process to be most important. The teacher is sometimes held up as the absolute model. This notion, of course, is fundamental. We do, initially, learn from imitation. However, learning must not cease there. In order for your child's personality to develop fully, he must be able to draw from his own experiences and develop his own imaginative powers. Children are not merely receptive beings. They are active beings, and should be treated as such. In this way, their imagination, the motivating power of their growth, will lead them to a constructive and not merely a complacent maturity.

Before I elucidate on the integration of culture and imagination, I would like first to discuss the nature and the origin of these imaginative powers. I believe that this will help us to further understand the full implications of the exercises presented in Level III.

To understand imagination, let's take a look at the reverse—the two-year-old's perception of reality. Considering that he has been in this crazy world for such a short time, he is doing remarkably well. He is a true scientist. He has an incredible ability to observe. Those things that offer him confusion are studied at an inexhaustible length. He empties the garbage, peruses the closets—all in attempts to fully understand their contents.

The two-year-old is actually more aware of his environment than many adults are. Most adults have developed highly intricate "screening" devices by the time they have children. If something is not immediately deserving of their attention, they ignore it. One day, on one of my numerous subway excursions with my daughter, 22 months old at the time, she kept insisting on the presence of "Mickey Mouse." I, of course, was absorbed in something else, and briefly glanced about, and assured her that there was no "Mickey Mouse." This remark did not daunt her. She tugged at me, jumped on me to get my attention. I looked about now more intently trying to deduce the cause of this clamor. Finally, I turned myself completely around, and there directly over my head hung an advertisement for an ice skating show with a picture of Mickey Mouse in all his splendor.

These kinds of events become commonplace. Your toddler is the first to notice the incongruous—clothing worn differently, furniture rearranged. His keen perceptions can often put us to shame. All of his reality orientations are in working order, with the exception of one—his conclusions about his observations and experiments. Without any knowledge of electronics, he decides that he is responsible for the lights coming on. His magic fingers flipped the switch! He does everything. He makes his windup toys move. He makes the little people dance on the television. There is no end to his powers.

With this power comes a tremendous amount of anxiety, even fear. For in this wonderful world where there are so many good things, there may be some awful things, too. The young child, unaware of the nature of causality, conjures up some frightening conclusions. Somewhere around the age of two or three, a child's sleep will be disturbed by nightmares of fierce animals, or perhaps of desertion by mommy or daddy. Most psychologists believe that the best way to relieve these fears is by playing imaginative games. By "going" places with him in the exercises, the small child can, on his own terms, come to deal with those things that frighten him. The zoo exercise, for instance, is a fabulous vehicle for relieving the child of his fear of wild animals, an extremely common phenomenon of toddlerhood. If your child is concerned about these plane rides you take for your business, take a little "plane trip" with him. My daughter, for example, had unusual anxiety about machines that made loud noises. She would cry or hide whenever I turned the blender on, took out the vacuum cleaner, or we passed by a power lawnmower. However, after many afternoons of machine building (see Level III, exercise #10), she began to help me take out the vacuum cleaner.

Now I am not suggesting that these exercises are a substitute for psychotherapy. The abovementioned anxieties are all within the normal range of child development. If there is any highly unusual anxiety, speak to your pediatrician. However, many simple fears can be overcome by using your child's imagination. And it is important that these fears be eliminated early in your child's life and in a comfortable environment. In this way, your child can learn that he can dictate his own fears and his own fantasies and not allow these fears or fantasies to consume him. His dealings with the frustrations of the real world are actually strengthened by his visits to fantasyland. We, as adults, do this by going to the movies or reading a novel. Everyone needs a rest. The world is not an easy place to live in, but it is the only place that would give us an extended lease. Your child's imagination is first developed as a protective device, a method of coping with his fears. Later, it is recognized as a means of enlarging and enriching his perceptions.

There are basic theories about the integration of the imagination and culture that need to be expounded: 1) that cultural elements can be understood at a far earlier age than has been presupposed, and 2) that the small child learns these concepts through the movement of his body. Now these are not my theories alone but those of the renowned early childhood educator, Maria Montessori. The more cultural material presented to the small child, the more he can learn. The "acting out" of social processes has a great meaning for the small child. He is able to imitate almost any of our daily functions. He combs his hair, shaves, scrubs the floors, and puts his dolls to sleep. These become necessary functions for him. They bring him closer to his world—his culture.

An African child may not need to go to the zoo as an American child may not need to hunt for his food. These concepts are not elements of his culture, though he may learn about them if they are adequately presented. The elements of any given culture are what enables us to function within a given society. These elements must be presented in a way that is meaningful to the child. Unfortunately, talking is not enough. We know ourselves, as adults, that no matter how vividly one can describe an event, it cannot replace first-hand experience. How then do you present culture to a small child and how then do you reinforce it? In a sense, you, as a parent, must create culture for your child. You must bring your child to culture and thus culture to your child. The best way is to bring it into your living room, where your child is comfortable and uninhibited. You are presenting the intangible in tangible terms—pictures he can see, music he can hear, movements he can feel in his body. This experience, though simulated, is very real to him. It is something with which he can identify.

I don't mean to devalue the importance of language or language skills. Language is possibly the most important element of culture we have. We could not function in Western society or any other society, for that matter, without language. However, language is only the culmination of many skills of which movement is the "mother." Most anthropologists have agreed that dancing or movement in any given culture is the foundation of the art of communication. The dance, itself, has been called the mother of the arts. Now what does this mean in terms of your toddler? You will notice that as your child's physical abilities develop, so does his vocabulary. True, the toddler may go through a silent period when he may concentrate solely on locomotor activity, but he often emerges from this period with a wealth of words that we could have never before imagined. It is as if he were a professor gathering information for his latest experiment. He refuses to divulge any of his material until he has sufficient data to substantiate his findings.

We do know one thing, however. The communication processes that are so vitally linked to the toddler period are preceded by some kind of motion. Very simply, large motor activities precede the finer motor activities. All neuromuscular functions begin in the spine, to which all of the nerves are attached. The muscles of speech as well as the muscles of running receive their stimulation from this point. The larger muscles develop before the smaller muscles. It is similar to building a sculpture out of clay. You first mold the clay into a satisfactory shape, then you work on the details. It is so with the child. He uses his larger muscles first and then refines his movement to include the more delicate muscles of speech. Without this thorough coordination, language would not take place. However, nonverbal communication is even more profound beyond the physical realm. The young child, whose language skills are not proficient, needs nonverbal outlets to release his feelings. These outlets can and should be constructive. It is far more creative for an adult to use his aggression on the tennis court than in the streets. Sociologists know this. That is why there are so many athletic programs sponsored in high-crime areas. Rather than suppressing your child's feelings or "curbing his nature" as they say, why not channel all of this energy into something creative and meaningful. Your child's feelings, his personality, function at the center of his life. He needs acceptable ways to vent them. What better way than using these exercises. He can be who he is—you love him. His fears, his joys, can all be explored here—intimately.

Although I feel that these exercises should be used to establish a warm bonding between parent and child, I also feel that the child's need for independence cannot be overlooked. When a child takes his first steps, he is truly severing the umbilical cord. Yet he is not without fear or hesitation. There is a kind of unwritten morality where independence is concerned. Yes, go off on your own but do everything the way that I told you to. The child, and especially the adolescent, is constantly battling for his own life versus the loss of parental love. Now we need parental love, and the removal of it, temporarily, to learn right from wrong. Some may argue that the child must know that he is loved at all times no matter what he does. This is true yet the parent must in some way adequately indicate disapproval of certain acts, or the toddler will feel that there is absolutely nothing that he cannot do. He loses respect for things. When a child learns that there are certain things that he prefers and other things that you do not, he also learns that you are a person, just like him. For a long time you were simply this all-providing force that swam through his life—all powerful, all good. Children need to understand that their parents are people.

On the other side of the coin (I mentioned this earlier in Level II), a child needs to understand that although his perception of things may be different, in some instances, it is not wrong. This is an extremely important lesson to teach your child. Most parents want to love their children and children want to love their parents. No one instinctively sets out to dislike someone. However, children mature into well-intentioned adults and still can't speak honestly with their parents because they are afraid they will hurt their feelings. We all know instances of this in our own families.

I don't favor complete disclosure of all family secrets, but I do favor the concept of choices being presented very early in childhood. I also favor recognizing individual differences and preferences positively. We all can't think the same way. It would be a pretty dull world. We are all guilty of being narrow from time to time. We go through life reserving suggestions or solutions for fear of being rejected.

This concept of a loving but separate existence is essential to your child's identity. I urge all parents to remember this when presenting these exercises. You, in a sense, are just the "key monitor." You hold the keys to open certain doors for your child, yet once he has gone through the passageway, it is his own adventure. This kind of love teaches your child to be himself—to be the best self he can be. These good healthy confident feelings will travel through adulthood with him.

Finally, I want to say that movement is not at the periphery of your child's life. It is at its center. Nourish your child's beginnings. Make them rich and exuberant. For in this, you will truly see the joy and challenge of parenting.

Level III: The Exercises

1. "My Talking Drum"

OBJECTIVE: to introduce musical concepts, identification of note values, and tempo

MATERIALS NEEDED: Mary Wigman drum (see below), index cards with note values drawn on them

DESCRIPTION: For the exercise, you will need a large drum. The best is what is known as a Mary Wigman drum (the cost is approximately $15), named for the modern dancer. The reason for this is that it comes with a large soft-tipped mallet, easy to handle and safer than traditional drumsticks. If not, try to have an ethnic style drum, African or Indian, which your child can beat upon with his hands. Whatever you choose, make sure it has a clear resonating sound. This is imperative so that your child will be able to distinguish the five separate note values.

Sit down on the floor with your child and your drum. Slowly begin to beat the drum. It doesn't matter what you play—just get his attention. He will want to beat the drum as well. Allow him to experiment.

You will have five colorful index cards prepared with the note values drawn on them. The note values are presented as follows:

     o   d   ♩   ♪   ♬

whole note   half note   quarter note   eighth note   sixteenth note

Tell your child these are called "notes"—"musical notes." Musical notes are special drawings that tell us how to make music.

Start with the whole notes. Tell him the whole note is very, very slow—the slowest of all the notes. The whole note is going to tell you what special way to make the drum "talk."

Pick up your mallet with your hand and beat out the following pattern four times, beating only on the count of 1 each time.

1 2 3 4 5 6 7 8
BEAT—hold for seven more counts.

Count out loud as you beat. It may help, for emphasis, if you increase your vocal volume on the count upon which you beat. For instance:

1 2 3 4 5 6 7 8
"ONE" loud—whisper for seven more counts.

Have your child count along with you if he hasn't taken the initiative yet, and either beat on the drum with you or clap his hands. Give him the mallet and the drum. Encourage him to repeat the same rhythm.

Tell him you would like him to dance a special whole note dance. Get yourself up to demonstrate. Start with a simple body shape. (See Level II.)

CODE: B—beat on the drum
        CYS—assume a new shape
        H—don't beat on the drum, pause; or hold the
           shape or position you assumed.

Begin to count out loud 1-2-3-4-5-6-7-8. On the first count, take your shape and hold it for seven more counts. When you approach the second phrase of counts, change your body shape on the "one" count and hold it for seven more counts. Repeat this about eight times. The rhythm should be as follows:

1	2	3	4	5	6	7	8
CYS	H	H	H	H	H	H	H

Use your body in as many ways as possible—stand, crouch, kneel, lie down. Be inventive! Your child should begin to mimic you at this point, though he may not be accurate in his timing. Continue to count out loud. Encourage him to proceed by himself. Pick up the drum and beat it in the previous pattern. When you have practiced this exercise several times, your child should be able to complete four eight-count phrases accurately.

The same procedure can be used for the four remaining note values. The beating patterns for each note is as follows. Tell your child that as you go along, the notes and his dances will become faster and faster.

half note	1	2	3	4	5	6	7	8
	B	H	H	H	B	H	H	H
	CYS				CYS			

Beat on your drum or strike your shape, then hold for three more counts. On the "five" count, change your shape and hold for three more counts. Repeat seven additional eight-count phrases.

quarter note	1	2	3	4	5	6	7	8
	B	H	B	H	B	H	B	H
	CYS		CYS		CYS		CYS	

You will be beating on the drum or striking a position every other count. Complete eight full eight-count phrases.

eighth note	1	2	3	4	5	6	7	8
	B	B	B	B	B	B	B	B
	CYS	CYS	CYS	CYS	CYS	CYS	CYS	CYS

There are no holds here. Every count demands a drumbeat or a change in body position. You will have to move quickly. Again complete eight full eight-count phrases.

sixteenth note	1	2	3	4	5	6	7	8
	BB	BB	BB	BB	BB	BB	BB	BB
	CYS	CYS	CYS	CYS	CYS	CYS	CYS	CYS
	CYS	CYS	CYS	CYS	CYS	CYS	CYS	CYS

The best way to demonstrate this is to say the sixteenth note is the fastest note—the running note. You should beat on the drum as fast as you can. When it is time to move, you can either run around the room or shake your body all over. Theoretically, you should be beating twice on the drum or changing your shape on every count. The drumbeating can be done with some degree of accuracy. However, it is unrealistic to assume we can move that quickly and accurately at the same time. As long as your child receives the general concept, it is not necessary to achieve perfection.

When you feel your child has understood these five note values (this will need to be practiced many times on separate occasions), you can play a special game with him. Tell him that the drum is ready to talk to him and tell him how to dance. Begin to beat out the separate note values on the drum in the manner described previously. See if he can identify the note values through using his body shapes. When he has become secure in this, begin to mix the note values. For instance, beat out a single quarter-note pattern followed by two whole-note patterns. Continue to count out loud. Surprise him! The change in tempos is exciting to small children though they won't often make a smooth transition. Be patient. Allow him to make mistakes. Remember, he learns from his errors.

2. "I Make the Drum Talk"

OBJECTIVE: to further enhance sound and music perception
MATERIALS NEEDED: Mary Wigman drum
DESCRIPTION: Use the drum again, as in exercise 1. Sit down
   with your child on the floor. Take the drum and begin to
   experiment with it. Don't be concerned with the actual
   note values in this exercise. We are trying to broaden our
   musical vocabulary here. In the beginning play simple
   rhythms. Slowly integrate more complex rhythms. For
   instance, start beating an even 1-2-3-4. (You do not need
   to vocalize in this exercise.) Now beat one sustained
   count, followed by three quick sharp beats. You are
   allowed to combine in any way you choose. You do not
   even have to keep standard eight-count phrases.
   Give the drum to your child. Have him do as you did—
   starting with the simple rhythms and broadening to the
   more complex rhythms.
   After he is finished, tell him you want to play a special
   game called "drum talk." Beat out a rhythm on the drum.
   See if your child can repeat it. Go slowly. Try to have him
   repeat at least four distinct musical patterns. Don't get
   too fancy. He is not ready.
   Hand the drum back to him. Tell him you want him to
   make the drum talk to you now. You will try to copy the
   sound. This game can be played back and forth for an
   indeterminate amount of time.

3. "I Make the Music/I Make the Dance"

OBJECTIVE: to develop the concepts of giving, receiving, responsibility and cooperation

MATERIALS NEEDED: several toy musical instruments (e.g., see below)

DESCRIPTION: You can do this alone with your child, but it is also a great deal of fun when he has friends visiting. You may use the same drum you did in exercises 1 and 2, though at this point I deem it rewarding to supplement with new instruments—toy cymbals, maracas, harmonicas. The children should be paired in couples. You are always available as a partner, if need be. Each couple receives one instrument of their choice.

Tell them one of the pair is going to be the musician and the other the dancer. The musician is going to play music for the dancer. Each musician is encouraged to play his own "musical selection" alone. You may demonstrate a particular musical rendition of your own on your chosen instrument. Have one of the musicians play something for you. Begin to dance to the music in your own way. Now encourage the dancer to follow suit. Each couple should have a chance to perform alone.

Now reverse the entire process. Have the musician become the dancer and the dancer, the musician. This exercise can be expanded by changing partners or having two musicians play for one dancer or two dancers perform with one musician playing. There are innumerable combinations for this exercise. Be courageous and experiment!

4. "The Waltz"

OBJECTIVE: to introduce the concept of waltz or three-four timing; to introduce the concept of continuous motion
MATERIALS NEEDED: recording of Johann Strauss waltzes
DESCRIPTION: You will need to be prepared with auditory aids for this exercise. First, I suggest, for all of the exercises to have a portable record player. The best waltz music, I feel (and so do other "highly discriminating tastes") is that of Johann Strauss. Go to your local classical record outlet or to the library (there are many such stores) and purchase several of his compositions. (e.g., the "Blue Danube," the "Emperor Waltz," etc.). This music is familiar and children respond readily to it.

This may be as good a time as any to introduce the concept of "composer" or music composition to your child. Tell him that composers are men and women who think about music or songs in their heads. These are not music or songs that they have heard before, but new music and songs that they have thought of all by themselves. Composers have to write these songs or music down so they can remember them. They do this by using the musical notes or special drawings that we talked about in exercises 1-3.

A man named Johann Strauss was a composer. He lived a long time ago in a country far away. Johann Strauss knew how much people loved to dance, and decided to write special dancing music. The special dance that people liked to do was called the waltz and the special music Mr. Johann Strauss wrote was called waltz music. This special waltz dance has three steps.

Count 1-2-3. Begin to clap "one-two-three" with your hands. Have your child do the same.

Now go to the record player and put on some of Mr. Strauss's music. Doesn't it sound wonderful? Mr. Strauss wrote very happy music for people to dance to, didn't he? Ask your child how he would like to dance to this music. Allow him to perform for you. In most instances, his movements will be soft, flowing, generally round. Join him if you like. Again, try to lead him discreetly into the three different spaces so that his dance is not restricted to the standing posture. Remember, we are not teaching the actual waltz steps here, we are trying to explore the waltz as a sound and as a subsequent feeling in the body. Getting down on the floor and rolling on the carpet is perfectly legitimate. Exchange roles at what you feel is an appropriate time, and have your child lead you through his waltz dance.

5. "Magic Words"

OBJECTIVE: to teach the concept of sequential motion—that one idea/movement precedes or follows another

DESCRIPTION: Tell your child that you want to play a special game with him called "the Magic Words." One of the magic words you have been thinking about is the word "stretch." How can you stretch with your body? Can you stretch an arm or a leg? The whole body can stretch long just like a rubber band. You can do this either standing up or lying down. Have your child join you and both of you can stretch together.

You have also thought about some other magic words like "spin," "run," and "jump." Perform each of these actions along with your child. Now tell him that you are going to put these magic words together to make a dance. How about these magic words—"run," "stretch," and "fall down?" Demonstrate this. Run to the other side of the room (or yard, if you are lucky enough to be outside), stretch long like a rubber band and fall to the floor. Have your child do the same. You can repeat this sequence several times.

Try another combination. How about "jump," "spin," and "make a shape." Again, jump across the room, spin in a circle, and make a shape with your body. Have your child imitate this sequence. If you feel that your child is ready, you may lengthen the sequence by adding another action. For instance, let's run, Jump, Spin, and fall to the floor. You can easily change the dynamics of a combination by simply altering the sequence—spin, jump, fall to the floor, and "get up and run."

Introduce new magic words—"leap," "hop," "crawl," and "slide"—the list is endless and so are their combinations. The number of actions given in a combination can grow to include six separate activities. Of course, there can be more, but then your child will begin to become confused and thus frustrated in his attempts.

Just remember these three simple rules:

1) Always introduce a magic word by demonstrating it with your body. 2) When presenting a new sequence, make sure you have demonstrated all of the magic words contained beforehand. 3) Always demonstrate the sequence by yourself first so that your child will know what is expected of him.

If you follow these rules, you and your child are sure to have a rewarding adventure. When you feel he is ready, allow your child to invent his own magic word sequences.

6. "The Playground"

OBJECTIVE: to introduce your child to narrative stories and their dramatization; to reinforce verbal skills and spatial concepts

DESCRIPTION: This exercise is particularly effective on a rainy day when a trip to the playground is not feasible. Make sure, however, on previous excursions to the playground, that you have explored all of the equipment available.

Now on this rainy day, you can tell your child that even though you can't go to a real playground, you can pretend that there is a playground right here in your living room (or whatever room you choose).

First, let's think about what there is in a playground. There are swings, seesaws, and slides. Discuss these with your child. Make sure that he is familiar with the general motion involved with each of these pieces of equipment. For instance, the swing goes back and forth, the seesaw goes up and down, etc.

Let's go on the swing first. Mommy or Daddy is going to go on the swing and you are going to push. Stand up and have your child stand directly in back of you. Tell him to give you a push, the way you do when he is on the swing. Let him push you. When he does, run slightly forward, then reverse, run backward until you are directly in front of him again. Tell him to push you again. Repeat the same action running back and forth. After a few pushes, your child, more than likely, will want a turn on the "swing." Reverse positions—this time with him standing directly in front of you. Give him a push and allow him to run forward. He is going to be reluctant at first to run backward. Take one of his hands and guide him slowly backward. Repeat this several times until he is comfortable doing this alone. Exchange roles several times and then go to "visit" something else.

Let's take a ride on the seesaw. How does the seesaw move? You must communicate to your child that although the seesaw itself goes up and down, both partners on the seesaw do not go up and down at the same time. One partner is up while the other is down. This will be difficult for him to comprehend at first. Take both of his hands and face him. Start simply, both of you bending your knees and straightening them at the same time. When he seems comfortable with this, introduce the concept of alternating the motion. Keep your knees straight but have him bend his knees. As he straightens his knees, bend yours. Do this very slowly. Explain to him that this is the way the seesaw moves. Repeat this several times.

Then go to the "slide." Ask your child what you do when you go on a slide. You climb the stairs, sit, and slide all the way down. Let's try that together. Stand next to each other and simulate the climbing action. Perhaps designate the number of steps on the slide—6 steps for example. Count 1-2-3-4-5-6, while you are climbing the steps. When you both have arrived at the top of the slide, have him sit down while you stand in back of him.
(NOTE: this part of the exercise must be done on a smooth uncarpeted surface. If this surface is wooden, make sure it is highly sanded and polished with no exposed splinters.)

Hold your child firmly, one hand bracing his shoulder girdle, the other supporting the base of his spine. Gently slide him across the floor, pushing him from behind. If he requests that you change roles, with him having to push you across the floor, do not deny him. When it is time for him to push you, help him by using your hands, legs, feet, whatever you need to maneuver yourself across the floor.

7. "The Zoo"

OBJECTIVE: to further foster the interpretation of narrative stories; to introduce your child to different animals; to reinforce the concepts of shape; to introduce the concepts of slow and fast, big and small; to reinforce verbal skills

MATERIALS NEEDED: pictures of wild animals (see below), or a picture book of wild animals

DESCRIPTION: Again, you will have to make a trip to the library or go to your old *National Geographics*. Gather pictures of wild animals, choosing species that are decidedly different from each other. For example, a tiger and a lion would not be appropriate together as choices since their physical interpretations are too similar. A good set of choices would be: an elephant, a lion, a monkey, and a snake. All of these animals are highly distinctive.

Either carefully mark your place in your book or paste the appropriate pictures on construction paper. Tell your child that you are going to make a little visit to the zoo (the pretend zoo, not the real one). Again, make sure your child has been to the real zoo beforehand.

Assemble your books and pictures and sit down on the floor and examine them. Show him a picture of an elephant. What does the elephant look like? An elephant is very big, very heavy, and he walks very slowly. The elephant has a long funny nose called a trunk. He swings his trunk back and forth when he walks. He uses his trunk to drink water and eat food much in the same way we would use a spoon. Let's see if we can move like an elephant. Stand up and begin to move slowly across the room transferring your weight from one leg to the other, loping from side to side. Keep your knees relaxed but do not bend them completely. The elephant is not a nimble animal—his agility is practically nonexistent. His strength comes from his size and his weight, not from his speed. Communicate these concepts with the languorous movements of your body. Clasp your hands together, lace your fingers, and keep your elbows straight to simulate the elephant's trunk. Swing your arms side to side, still keeping your arms straight, as you lumber across the room.

Now let's visit the lion. What is the lion like? Again, show your child the picture. The lion is big, strong, and furry. He has a loud fierce roar. How does the lion move? He is certainly faster than the elephant. Get down on all fours and begin to crawl at a moderate pace. Toss your head and open your mouth widely. Go ahead and roar.

Let's go see the monkey now. Show your child the monkey's picture and question him about the monkey. The monkey is a very friendly, funny animal. He likes to swing from trees. Sometimes he even scratches himself and makes silly faces. How do you think the monkey likes to move? The monkey, unlike the elephant, is an incredibly agile animal. He jumps and hops, jiggles his torso, and contorts his face. Here is your chance to be a real "ham."

Lastly, let's visit the snake. Show your child the picture and again question him. What is the snake like? He is long and thin and crawls on his belly. He has a long thin tongue that he likes to stick out of his mouth. Go ahead, get down on the floor and crawl.

After you have completed your zoo visit be sure to question your child on his adventure. Which animal was the biggest, the funniest? Which one did he like the best, the least? Why does he feel this way? The same zoo animals can be visited again and again and there will always be something new about them.

8. "Wheels and Wings"

OBJECTIVE: to teach your child the various methods of transportation; to reinforce narrative stories and their dramatization; to develop the awareness of shape and spatial concepts

DESCRIPTION: This exercise is especially effective and rewarding when done prior to an extended trip. Children are apprehensive, though curious, about prolonged outings. Talk to your child. Tell him that people come and go all day long. Mommy and Daddy get to work in the morning by driving the car. He himself may be picked up by a bus to go to nursery school. If you live in a large metropolitan area, you can discuss mass transit—the infamous subways. Sometimes people like to go far, far away. They like to go to places that they have never been before—beautiful places, exciting places. Then they can take a boat or a plane. Again, always have pictures available.

Let's take a ride in the car (the pretend car) right here in the living room. Go over to the car, open the door, and climb in. Sit down on the floor adjacent to your child. Tell him that you are in a special car, you are going to let him drive. Now what does Daddy or Mommy do when they drive the car? They put the key in the "ignition" and turn on the car's motor. Then they press one of the pedals on the floor with their foot. Then they put both hands on the steering wheel and off they go. As you are "driving," ask your child what he "sees"—trees, houses—perhaps he sees a few of his friends. Encourage conversation and imagination.

You can take a ride on the subway or bus in much the same fashion. You can sit on your couch and gently bounce on your buttocks to simulate the jolting motion of these modes of transportation.

Locomotives are especially fun. I recommend *being* the locomotive rather than just riding in one. The two of you can stand up, one directly in back of the other. Shuffle your feet and make a good old-fashioned tooting sound. You are never too old to enjoy this.

It is also more effective to be an airplane rather than just an airplane passenger. This is simply because there is more movement available to you. You can crouch on the floor with both of your knees bent, stand up on tiptoe and "take off" with both of your arms spreadeagled.

Again, converse with your child. Talk about the different places you can go and how you are going to get there. Which is his favorite ride?

9. "Windup Toys"

OBJECTIVE: to further explore the relationship of shape and spatial concepts; to reinforce the dramatization of narrative stories; to teach the concept of controlled movement; to teach the concept of the acceleration and the deceleration of motion

MATERIALS NEEDED: several different windup toys

DESCRIPTION: Go into your child's toybox or a nearby novelty store and pick out a few "mechanical favorites." Children, through the decades, have always been fascinated by windup toys. Take these "finds" out and sit down with your child to discuss them. He probably knows already how this piece of equipment works. Tell him to show you the toy. After he has wound it up and it has done its "dance," ask him about it. How does this toy move? Guide him through the concept that after the toy is wound, it first moves very quickly, then it moves slower and slower until it stops.

Does he think he could move like a windup toy? Tell him that you are going to take a little walk to the pretend toy store to look for some special windup toys. Open the door to the toy store and walk in. Tell him that you see a wonderful windup toy soldier (or whatever). How does the soldier move? The soldier is very straight. He marches "1-2-3-4." You want to be this soldier windup toy. Would he (your child) help you? Tell your child that there is a special key in your back that you want him to turn. Stand very tall and allow your child to turn the key. Now begin to march in a highly exaggerated fashion, lifting your knees high and swinging your arms. Slowly begin to "wind down" until you stop. Ask your child if he wants to be the soldier now. Undoubtedly, he will. Have him stand tall and straight while you wind him up with the key. Have him march around a bit and then tell him that the soldier is getting tired and is going to move slower and slower until he stops. You may repeat this until your child is satisfied.

I would introduce two other windup toys just to contrast the qualities of motion. I like to use the ballerina and the clown. The ballerina, I present in the true music box tradition—"tippie-toeing," twirling about. Add your own embellishments if you care to. The clown is more clumsy. He may make funny faces. His movements are loose and pendulous in nature.

Always demonstrate the character first, but don't insist upon replication. As long as your child gets the general idea, "it's OK." Take turns frequently, one being the toy and the other, the winder. Make sure he understands the idea of dancing slowly as opposed to dancing quickly, and the connection between these two concepts.

10. "Let's Build a Machine"

OBJECTIVE: to foster the integration of shape, spatial, and auditory concepts

DESCRIPTION: Take your child to a construction site one afternoon and let him take a good look through one of the holes in the fence. Ask him to look at the machinery and see how it works. There are wheels, bars, screws, and chains. These machines can move in many ways. Most of the sounds they make are very loud.

When you come home, tell your child that there are some machines right here in the house. You have a vacuum cleaner, a sewing machine, a typewriter. All of these machines move and make sounds. They all move in different ways and their sounds are different. Some machines have very loud sounds, others are quieter. All machines move and make sounds at the same time.

Does he think he could move and make a sound like a machine with his body? If he is dismayed, demonstrate. It does not matter specifically what you do, as long as it is angular and rotary in nature. In other words, a smooth flowing motion would not be appropriate for demonstrating a machine but almost any other motion would be acceptable. Also keep your movement stationary so that you move within a given space rather than in a locomotor way. Now have your child do his interpretation. Tell him you are going to make your machine and make a sound for it. Make a sound while you are being your machine. Have him do the same with his machine.

Now you are going to build a machine together. Have him become his machine (movement and sound together). Once he gets going, attach yourself to him in some way—put your hand on his shoulder, lie down on the floor and hold his ankle—and make your machine. Have it so the two movements and the two sounds are being created simultaneously. You may repeat this exercise countless times and never do the same machine twice.

NOTE: The sound made may either be vocal or made by slapping parts of the body.

11. "The Story of Autumn"

OBJECTIVE: to explore the integration of color, music, shape, cultural elements, and verbal skills

MATERIALS NEEDED: Several pictures of autumn scenes, a recording of light classical music, some leaves gathered from outside

DESCRIPTION: It is best to introduce this exercise during autumn. Children are literal and respond better when their learning process is being reinforced by what is occurring environmentally. To present this concept during another season would be remote and not as readily accepted.

Before presenting this exercise, rummage through your supply of old magazines. Find several autumn pictures, cut them out, and paste them on colored construction paper. If you are particularly industrious, go outside and gather leaves: fresh green leaves, orange leaves, and gray withered leaves. Sit down on the floor close to your child. Have some music playing. It doesn't have to be anything in particular—just atmosphere music. Talk to your child. Find out what he knows about autumn. Most small children have observed the trees. Tell him that in the spring, leaves grow on the trees and in the autumn, about which you'd like to tell him a special story, these leaves change to beautiful colors, are blown from the trees by the wind, and then fall slowly to the ground. Some trees have big leaves, some small. Some trees have very dark brown bark, others have bark that is almost white. There are so many different kinds of trees—some even grow fruit. You can either take him over to the window and look at the trees outside or show him the pictures you have pasted.

Ask him what tree he likes the best. Ask him to make the tree shape with his body. You may show him with your own body. You are allowed to be traditional in your own demonstration. Stand up, tall and erect, and spread your arms wide. After he shows you his tree, quiz him about it. Is it a big tree, a strong tree, a pretty tree? Ask him to show you with his body how big, how strong, how pretty.

Tell him you are thinking of a special tree—a tree you would like to become; a strong beautiful apple tree. If you have a picture of this tree, show it to him. Use your body to communicate this strong beautiful "apple tree image." Relate to the background music. It may be helpful to you. Now ask your child if he has a special tree to show you. He may, more than likely, demonstrate and verbalize simultaneously. This is fine. His imagination may overwhelm you and make little sense—he may tell you of a big, scary, purple tree that looks like his dog, Spot. Allow for this personal expression. It is natural and good for him. He has all the time in the world to learn the traditional responses. He will edit his material later. It is important that he expresses himself now in a way he feels comfortable and accepted. Praise his "tree" liberally and ask him to show you more. You may introduce a few new trees of your own.

Show him the leaves you found. Tell him that the wind blows the leaves from the tree. Ask him to become a leaf ready to be blown. You will be the wind, and he, the leaf. Have him stand up and make a "leaf shape" with his body. Start making some typical wind noises with your mouth—blowing and hissing. You may need to take his hands the first few times you do this and twirl around in a circle until you both fall softly to the floor. The "softness" may be difficult to achieve, if not impossible. Children tend to be indelicate. When he becomes secure, he can whirl about by himself and tumble to the floor. It is also good for him to become the wind a few times and blow your leaf off the tree. Music should continue throughout this exercise.

When you've both taken turns being the leaf and the wind, tell him that the two of you are two leaves on the same big tree. Make your leaf shapes together. Now the big imaginary wind comes and sends the two of you whirling around the room and onto the floor. Children love this! It is great excitement!

Take out your leaves again. Show him a fresh new leaf and an old brown withered leaf. Let him feel the leaves—how they differ in texture. He can see how their colors differ. The green leaf is smooth, bright, pretty. The brown leaf is old, dry, it crumbles when you squeeze it with your hand—like a cookie crumbles. Ask him to show you how the bright, pretty, green leaf makes him feel with his body. Dance with him, if you wish. Now ask him to show you with his body how the dry leaf makes him feel. Again, dance along with him. There are no set movements to be executed here. However, there is a distinction to be learned. The green leaf dance should be smoother, flowing, perhaps lyrical, happy. The brown leaf dance, in contrast, should be slower, the shape more angular, tight—a sadder dance.

Now for the *pièce de résistance*—leaf raking. If you live in an urban area, it may be necessary to have pictures of people raking leaves. After you have discussed the leaf raking with your child, get out your imaginary rakes and begin to rake all those brown withered leaves into big piles. You can put your rakes down, and just gather the leaves into your arms and throw them onto the pile. Remember, these motions must be highly exaggerated to be understood. Don't be afraid to get "into it." The more elaborate your presentation, the more your child can enjoy this.

Once you have all the leaves raked, tell your child you are going to run and jump into the pile. We all have memories of this. Try to recollect. It may help to get several cushions arranged in the center of the floor as buffers. You will have to approach this gingerly, especially if you live in an apartment building. Hold hands, run or skip, and jump into the pile of leaves. You will have to repeat this many times. It has an addictive effect. When the two of you drop into the pile, roll, and kick your legs. Your child will most likely be howling and squealing. Within reason, howl and squeal with him.

If you live in the country or have access to a park, it is great fun to do this exercise outdoors. The experiences reinforce each other.

12. "Spring Words"

OBJECTIVE: to foster the integration of narrative stories and their dramatization; to explore cultural elements, verbal skills, shape, space, and color; to introduce the concept of birth and new beginnings

MATERIALS NEEDED: several pictures of spring themes (see below), baby-animal picture book, a package of flower seeds

DESCRIPTION: As with autumn, this exercise is best presented during the season it represents.

Go through your old magazine supply and find some appropriate pictures of spring—colorful foliage, bees, birds, blooming trees, and newborn animals (you may want to go to the library and take out a baby animal book). Paste all of the magazine pictures on construction paper. Tell your child that you want to talk to him about the springtime. The spring is such a lovely time of year. Everything is new and beautiful. The flowers bloom, the trees blossom with fresh green leaves. The spring is the time when baby animals are born.

Show him the pictures you have gathered. Tell him to look particularly at the flowers. Flowers are so beautiful. They come in many shapes and colors. There are very large flowers and very tiny flowers. Does he know where flowers come from? Flowers come from very small beads called "seeds." He has seen seeds before (if you are able to purchase a small package of flower seeds, show them to him). You have used them when you were cooking—perhaps some sesame or caraway seeds, the kind that are in rye bread.

When you want a flower to grow, you dig a little hole in the ground, place the seed in the hole, cover the seed with dirt, and pat the dirt with your hand. Then you water that little seed, because both seeds and flowers need water to drink just like you and me. He has seen you water the plants and flowers in your home and perhaps in the garden.

Flowers also need sunshine. The sunshine is like food to the plants and flowers. After a few weeks or months, when the seed has gotten enough water and sunshine, it begins to grow very slowly. The little sprout will have something called a "bud." The bud contains the beautiful colorful petals of the flower. Soon after that the bud will open up and the full beautiful flower will bloom. Does he think he could be the little seed growing into the big flower with his body? Tell him that you are going to try this.

Take some pretend seeds in your hand. You are going to plant them right here in your living room. Dig some little holes with your fingers and place the seeds in them. Cover them up with soil and pat the dirt with your hands. Go get your watering can (the pretend watering can) and water these little seeds. Now crouch down on the floor in a fetallike position. Tell him that you are the little seed now and need to be watered. Have your child water you. Very slowly, begin to grow. Kneel and slowly rise to standing with your arms overhead. Now "blossom." Open your arms widely and make a flower shape with your body.

Now tell your child that you want him to be the little seed. Have him get down on the floor and curl up into a little ball. Get your watering can and water him. Tell him to show you with his body how that little seed grows into a big beautiful flower. After he shows you this, try it together. Perhaps have some soft music playing in the background and perform some "dancing flowers" together.

Take out your baby animal book and look at it with your child. Ask him what he knows about baby animals. What are some baby animal names? What about "kitten," "puppy," and "calf." What, for instance, does the kitten do? Can he show you with his body? You can join this activity, guiding him as you go. The little kitten licks his paws and crawls. When he gets angry, he may scratch.

Demonstrate these activities and have your child volunteer new activities.

You can go through this procedure with a number of baby animals. When your child has made several baby animals, you can try this: Each of you will choose a baby animal to become, and then the two baby animals can play together. My favorite way to end this particular exercise is to have both baby animals play until they are both very tired. Then they can go to a comfortable corner, curl up, and go to sleep. This is especially effective right before naptime.

13. "Summer Feelings"

OBJECTIVE: to foster the integration of shape, space, color, and narrative stories and their dramatization

MATERIALS NEEDED: some light classical background music, pictures of summer scenes, pictures of shells or real shells

DESCRIPTION: Do find some appropriate background music. Again, present this exercise during the summer. This exercise is especially refreshing on a rainy day when visits to the beach or other outings are not possible. If you do not live near the shore, it is especially important to have pictures of shore areas on hand.

Ask your child about the summer. How does he feel about it? Summer is very hot—the hottest of all the seasons. Because it is so hot, you can become very lazy and sleepy. Everything seems to be so slow in the summer.

To cool off, we go to the beach (if you do not live nearby, present the pictures). Here it is not so hot, and the water is nice and cool. Maybe we could take a pretend trip to the beach.

Take off your shoes and wander over the living room carpet or playroom floor. Wiggle your toes in the "sand." The sand is so warm and white. Let's find a nice spot on the sand to sit. Sit down on the sand. Perhaps take out a pretend tube of suntan lotion and rub it on each other's backs. The sun is very hot and sometimes it can burn our skin. That is why we put our lotion on first. Let's take a good look at the sun. What shape is the sun? Can you make that sun shape with your body? Make the sun shape yourself and have your child do the same. Can you make that sun shape in the high, the middle, and the low space? Try to make the sun shape in all of the three spaces.

Look at the pictures of the beautiful water. It is so blue and so cool. Look at the waves, how they roll onto the shore. Do you think that you can make a wave with your body? This motion can be done very simply by curling and uncurling the spine or by curling and uncurling an extremity. You can start with both knees bent, both feet flat on the floor. Bring your chest down to your knees, drop your head, and let your arms hang limp—sort of a standing fetal posture. Begin to shuffle slightly backward as you slowly uncurl your spine until you are standing. Now gently run forward, swing your upper body downward until your chest is once again over your knees. Repeat this several times, guiding your child through the sequence as you do so. This moving back and forth motion simulates the rolling motion of the waves.

Maybe now we can run down to the water and take a little swim. Run down to the water and jump in. If your child has not engaged in swimming classes as yet, demonstrate the standard swimming action—arms alternately reaching forward and swinging behind. If you like, you can hold his hands while he lies on his belly and kicks his feet. You can even play the ever popular "dive under the legs" game—each of you alternating, taking turns diving under each other's legs. (You may have a little difficulty diving under his legs, but do it anyway. Children love to see their parents struggle a little. It makes them more human, less distant.)

After you come out from your "dip," you may want to gather shells along the shore. Again, have visual aids prepared for this (either pictures of shells or the real thing). Shells come in a myriad of shapes and are fascinating to small children. Better yet, if you are in the habit of visiting the shore, develop a small shell collection for yourself and your child. After you have wandered about the living room carpet, stooping to pick up the "shells," sit down with your child and look at the shell representations you have gathered. Ask your child about the shells. What shape are they? Which ones are large? Which ones are the prettiest? Which ones are the sharpest? Tell your child that you are going to pick a shell you like and make it with your body in some way. Do that. Try to make this shape in the three different spaces. Have your child attempt the same thing. You can continue in this manner until all of the shells have been explored.

You can devise a variety of activities to engage in at the beach—building sand castles, playing beach ball, etc. Just remember to integrate the concepts of shape and space and above all the imagination.

14. "Winter Wonderland"

OBJECTIVE: to integrate the concepts of shape, space, color, and cultural elements; to reinforce verbal skills; to explore narrative stories and their dramatization

MATERIALS NEEDED: recording of Christmas music, snowflake "cutouts," pictures of winter scenes, pictures of ice skating

DESCRIPTION: This exercise is especially good to do before the first snow. Have the appropriate background music playing (Christmas tunes are effective). For your visual aids you will need either pictures or tissue cutouts of snowflakes, pictures of winter scenes, snowmen, sleds, ice skaters, etc. If it is a snowy day, you are in luck. If not, use your visual aids. Take your child over to the window and look at the snowflakes. See how pretty and silvery they are. Snowflakes melt and disappear so quickly. Do you know that there are no two snowflakes that are exactly alike? So many different shapes—so many different sizes. You have some pictures of snowflakes that you would like to show him. Spread the pictures out on the floor. You are going to pick one of these snowflakes and make its shape with your body. Again, make sure you make the shape in all of the three spaces. Tell your child that the snowflakes are never still, they are always being blown about by the wind. You are going to move, twirl about the room just like a snowflake. To finish, you may each choose a snowflake and twirl about in the wind together.

Maybe we can build a snowman. This does not require any skilled "mimemanship"—just get down on your knees and roll a snowball together. Put one snowball on top of the other and mime some fantastic embellishment—like a carrot for a nose, a couple of buttons for eyes. You can also lie down in the snow and "make angels"—swinging your arms and legs back and forth.

This part is my favorite—the dance of the ice skaters. Again, have some pictures ready. There are plenty of photos available of skating celebrities. When it is cold outside, a pond or a lake freezes—like water does in the refrigerator to make ice cubes. The water turns to ice and is so hard that people wearing special shoes called ice skates can get out on the ice and dance upon it. Have some waltz music playing—the child is already familiar with this and it is the most conducive skating music I have found.

You can get down on the floor and put on your pretend ice skates. Now go out onto the ice (uncarpeted bare floors are best), and begin to slide your feet, holding your child's hand. Try to keep in time to the music if you can—it will help your child establish the rhythm of skating. Once you get this skating motion under way, you can introduce many other "moves"—spins, turns on one foot. The potential here is enormous. Allow your child to create his own skating dance here. Children are very receptive to waltz music and your child should have no difficulty. You may have more trouble restraining him from flying around the room.

15. "The Nutcracker"

OBJECTIVE: to foster the integration of shape, space, verbal skills, and cultural elements

MATERIALS NEEDED: recording of the *Nutcracker Suite*, optional picture book of Nutcracker themes, a nutcracker, some nuts, a globe, pictures of a Russian, Chinese and Arabian dancer in traditional garb

DESCRIPTION: This is an especially good exercise to do with your child before you take him to this particular ballet. In this way, he will have some reference points. Children are always more receptive and more comfortable with those things with which they are familiar.

Again, take a little trip to your local discount record outlet or library and pick up a copy of the *Nutcracker Suite*. If you can find a coloring book or a small picture book dealing with this subject, all the better. If not, gather some pictures of ballet dancers and also three ethnic pictures: traditional Chinese, Arabian, and Russian peoples in ethnic dress. You should also have a nutcracker, a nut, and a world globe (if it is impossible to get the globe, you may use a map. However, children are very literal. If you are going to show them the locations of different countries, it is important for the child to understand the spherical nature of the world).

Tell your child that you want to tell him a story—a very special Christmas story (or simply, a fairy story, if you prefer). Have Tchaikovsky's music playing in the background and show your child the pictures. Before you begin the story of the *Nutcracker Suite*, tell your child about the composer. Refresh your child's memory by reinforcing the idea that a composer is a person who writes music with those special little notes. Tchaikovsky was a composer. He lived a long time ago in a country far away. This country is called Russia or the Soviet Union. It is very cold in Russia. Mr. Tchaikovsky decided one day to write music for a ballet. A ballet is a kind of play— perhaps he has seen one on television. The difference between a ballet and a play is that in the ballet, nobody talks, they tell their whole story by dancing. The name of the ballet that Mr. Tchaikovsky wrote is the *Nutcracker Suite*.

You can skim the story of the Nutcracker ballet by saying it is the story of a little girl named Clara. Clara's uncle brings her a beautiful nutcracker shaped like a soldier for Christmas. At night Clara dreams that the Nutcracker turns into a handsome prince and takes her to magical lands where she meets many friends who dance for her.

One of the friends she meets lives in the same country where Mr. Tchaikovsky lived, Russia. Show your child your picture of the Russian in traditional garb (dancing costume). Put on the Russian dance music. This music is quite emphatic and implies large masterful movements. Begin to demonstrate your Russian dancer— leaping, jumping, high kicks, deep knee bends—any large demonstrative movement is appropriate. Encourage your child to participate. Have him inaugurate his own big "Russian movements" (use all of the shapes and spaces. Show your child the countries on the globe).

After you have finished your Russian dance, show him your Chinese picture. The Chinese are polite and like to bow. Put on the Chinese dance music and begin your interpretation. Keep your steps small and simple—your jumps very quick and not too high. The extremities should be kept close to the body to help contrast with the wide overt movements of the Russian dancer. Again, remember your spaces. Do something high, middle, and low. When your child feels comfortable, he will join you.

The last dance is the Arabian dance. Again, show your child your Arabian dancer picture and the country of Arabia on the globe. They don't wear as many clothes when they are dancing like the Russians do. Their movements are very snakelike, round and slow and curvy. Put on the Arabian dance music. This may be your only opportunity to be a belly dancer so take full advantage. Roll your head, your shoulders, your hips, making wavelike movements with your arms. Use your different spaces, high, middle, and low. Encourage your child to participate.

After you have finished, ask your child which dance he has enjoyed the most. Replay that music and conclude with the both of you dancing his favorite dance.

16. "Christopher Columbus"

OBJECTIVE: to reinforce the integration of the concepts of shape, space, color, cultural elements; to introduce the concept of discovery

MATERIALS NEEDED: a globe, pictures of Christopher Columbus and his three ships

DESCRIPTION: This exercise should be done close to Columbus Day. Again, you will need plenty of visual aids—a globe, a picture of Christopher Columbus and his three ships. Sit down with your child and look at the globe. Show him where you live. Point to it on the globe and have your child do the same. See if he knows the country in which he lives. Tell him that you both live in the United States of America, though our country was not always called that. Many hundreds of years ago before he or anybody he knows was born, there lived in a country called Italy—show him Italy on the globe—a man whose name was Christopher Columbus. Christopher Columbus was very very smart and he knew things many other people didn't know. Christopher Columbus thought the world was round—just like the globe, but most people thought the world was flat—just like a pancake.

Christopher Columbus went to talk to the queen. Queen Isabella was her name. He wanted her to give him some money so he could take a trip around the world and prove the world was round.

Because everyone was so afraid to ride in their boats, people didn't even know about America. They didn't even know it was here. When Christopher Columbus took his trip, he found America! Because America was such a wonderful place, many, many people decided to ride in their boats and come to America to live.

Maybe we could pretend we are Christopher Columbus. We could build a large boat and travel across the ocean to find America. So let's get our pretend "tools"— our hammers and nails and screwdrivers and some wood and build our boat. Gather your "wood" and "tools" and mime your hammering and sawing. Build a big, big boat. What kind of shape is the boat? This boat has big sails. Sails are like big sheets. When the wind blows, the sails help move the boat.

Could he make the shape of this boat with his body? You are going to try this yourself. Stand tall, legs spread apart. Extend both of your arms. The wind blows and fills your sails. Move your body "with the wind," swaying to and fro like the mast of a ship. Ask your child to do the same. Maybe you can make a large boat with both of your bodies together. Both of you can stand tall, one in back of the other, legs slightly apart, arms extended, and wait for the wind to come. Sometimes the wind is very strong, sometimes, it is very gentle. Demonstrate the difference. A gentle wind would not make the body move very much, while a strong wind would greatly move the boat. Sometimes there is a powerful storm. The wind and the rain blow very hard—almost blow the boat over. Let's try that. Conclude by having the storm pass over and the boat becoming very still.

17. "Hallowe'en"

OBJECTIVE: to reinforce the integration of narrative stories and their dramatization; to explore verbal skills, music, and shape and spatial concepts

MATERIALS NEEDED: a recording of Dukas's "The Sorcerer's Apprentice," some traditional Hallowe'en pictures

DESCRIPTION: This exercise is best done on or close to Hallowe'en. I have found Dukas's "The Sorcerer's Apprentice" the most conducive of the Hallowe'en feeling. It is "spooky" without being too frightening. Try to also have some traditional Hallowe'en pictures—a pumpkin, a witch, a ghost.

Ask your child about Hallowe'en. What does he know? He must know about "trick or treat." Show him your Hallowe'en pictures. I usually choose a pumpkin, a witch, and a ghost (though other Hallowe'en characters are appropriate) because they are easily contrasted with each other.

Show him the pumpkin. What shape is the pumpkin? What color? If the pumpkin could dance, how would it move? Would he like to show you his pumpkin dance? Join him, if you like. Again, make sure he uses all the spaces, high, middle, and low. Suggest that the pumpkin might be happy, and do round, jumpy, happy movements.

When you have finished the pumpkin dance, bring out your picture of the witch. How is the witch different from the pumpkin? The witch is much straighter than the pumpkin and she is not so happy. Everything about her is very straight and "pointy"—her hat, her nose, the broom upon which she rides. Maybe he can show you a witch dance. Emphasize the straight shape of the witch as opposed to the round shape of the pumpkin. Join him in the witch dance, guiding him through all of the three spaces.

Lastly, show him the ghost. Ghosts are very smooth

and curvy. They move very slowly. Can he show you how a ghost moves with his body? Again join in his spooky ghost dance. Emphasize the curvy wavelike movements of the ghost and of course, the three spaces.

18. "The Indian Dance"

OBJECTIVE: to emphasize the integration of space, shape, cultural elements, color, and music

MATERIALS NEEDED: pictures of Indians and Pilgrims, some small percussive instruments

DESCRIPTION: Present this exercise close to Thanksgiving. Have some pictures of Indians and Pilgrims and some small percussive instruments available. There is no need to go through an elaborate discussion on the Pilgrims and Thanksgiving here. Religious persecution is something a small child cannot possibly understand. However, if you have adequately discussed Christopher Columbus (Exercise #16), your child will understand that people traveled to America because it was such a wonderful place. The Pilgrims, the people who came to live in America, took their boats to America to find a better place to live. When they arrived here, they met the Indians. The Indians were and are people who have lived in America a long time. They showed the Pilgrims how to plant food and how to build houses.

One beautiful day the Pilgrims and the Indians decided to have a big party. They brought all kinds of food and there was plenty of dancing. The Indians used to dance for just about everything. They had a sun dance, a rain dance, a war or angry dance, and a wedding dance. When they danced, they wore special costumes and painted their faces with brightly colored makeup, and used special music made only with drums.

Take out his drum and perhaps some small percussive instruments. Take one instrument yourself and give him one. Begin to beat out some simple rhythms (see Level III, Exercises #1-2-3 for examples of simple rhythms). Have him imitate this rhythm or perhaps invent one of his own. As you beat out the rhythm together, ask him what kind of dance he thinks this is. Does it sound like a sun dance, a rain dance? Once he has decided, have him show you this dance. Ask him what kind of shapes and spaces he can use to make this dance. Ask him if he would like to play the drum while you dance. Try to explore as many of the dances as you can—the rain dance, the war or angry dance, or the sun dance. Try to find movements that demonstrate these feelings. For example, light airy movement would constitute a sun dance, while strong powerful movement would be a war dance. Again, be sure to include all of the shapes and the spaces.

19. "Colors, Colors"

OBJECTIVE: to introduce the concept of color as it relates to movement

MATERIALS NEEDED: three pieces of construction paper—red, blue, and black

DESCRIPTION: Have three pieces of construction paper handy—red, blue, and black. These are the three colors you will be discussing with your child. I have chosen those colors as opposed to other available choices because they are the most highly representative of distinctive feelings. Black, of course, is not truly a color but the absorbtion of all color. This concept, however, is far too sophisticated for a small child to comprehend and since it does not distract from the focus of this exercise, I always include it. I also suggest that you find some appropriate music for each of the three colors. This music does not have to be specific as long as you have several varied types to indicate varied feelings—some angry music, some happy music, some scary music, some sleepy music.

I generally start by sitting down on the floor with the child and having a general discussion about color. What colors are in this room, for instance? Find out how many colors he knows. What kinds of things are green, what kind yellow, etc.?

Tell him that you would like to do some dances about color and that you would like him to help. You may start with any color that you wish. I generally start with the color red. Take out your piece of red construction paper. Have your child look at this color. What kinds of things are red? Fire engines, roses, and stop signs are red. How does he feel about the color red? You will get a variety of responses here. Just because you may feel that red is an angry color, do not expect your child to feel that way. Your child may feel that the color red is a happy, smiley, warm color. Try to solicit as many verbal descriptions as you can, e.g., red is hot, red is fiery, red is happy and round like an apple. Once you have established how he feels, accept your child's judgment and ask him to show you with his body a little dance about the color red. Put on some "red" music for him that corresponds to his particular red feeling.

Go through all of the colors in this manner, asking him what things are this color and then asking him how he feels about this color. Some typical responses for the color black may be: Black is dark and spooky, black is sad, black is big and strong. Blue responses m include: blue is quiet, blue is cool, blue is pretty. Any of these reactions is appropriate. Don't be afraid to include yourself in these discussions. You child may do a pretty blue dance. However, you may feel that blue is sad. It is important for small children to understand that different people have different feelings about the very same things. Alone with you, your child is learning acceptance. There is no right or wrong here—just differences.

20. "Paint the Music"

OBJECTIVE: to foster the total integration of shape, space, color, music, story telling, verbal skills, and art forms

MATERIALS NEEDED: shelving paper or newsprint paper, crayons or magic markers, recording of a classical composer

DESCRIPTION: Either have some blank shelf paper handy or go to your local crafts store and purchase those large neutral sheets of "newsprint" paper of which children are so fond. Get out your crayons or nontoxic magic marking pens and also a record or tape of an interesting musical selection. I often present a classical piece, one in which there are a number of emotional moods demonstrated. Bach, Beethoven, Mozart—these are all acceptable. Do try to use a composer who has not been addressed in previous exercises.

Spread the paper and the crayons on the floor, and get down on your hands and knees with your child. Tell him that you are going to play some very special music for him. You want him to listen to the music and think about how this music makes him feel. Does he feel happy, sad, silly, etc.? He is going to draw you a picture about how the music makes him feel and you are going to draw a picture about how the music makes you feel.

Put on the music and begin to draw. Try not to guide your child in any particular way. Allow him to draw whatever pleases him. One thing that may happen at first is that he may try to imitate what you are drawing. If this happens, explain to him that although the drawing he is making is very nice, you want a special drawing from him. One that you have never seen before. You want to be surprised. Continue this activity as long as your child's interest is held.

When you have both completed your drawings, shut the music off briefly and ask your child about the music and the drawing. How did the music make him feel? What did he think about while he was drawing? What kinds of things did he draw? Volunteer the same kind of information about your drawing. An example might be: This music made me think about the colors green and blue, and soft curvy shapes. This music made me feel quiet and sleepy. Of course, your child's initial reaction will never be as sophisticated as your own, but do listen. He may surprise you.

When you have fully discussed and exchanged your feelings about the music and the drawings, tell your child that you want to make a special dance about the music and the drawings. How does the music and the drawing make his body feel? Does he think he could show you? Turn on the music and let him dance. If he has difficulty, talk to him about the shapes and the spaces. Can he go fast or slow? To conclude, join him in your own interpretation—both of you dancing the music and the drawings, together.

Bibliography

1. Axline, Virginia M. *Play Therapy*. New York: Ballantine Books, 1969.

2. Clive, Geoffrey *The Philosophy of Nietzsche*. New York: Signet, 1965.

3. Eibesfeldt, Eibl *Love and Hate*. New York: Holt, Rinehart, and Winston, 1971.

4. Erikson, Erik H. *Childhood and Society*. New York: W. W. Norton and Company, 1950.

5. Fraiberg, Selma H. *The Magic Years*. New York: Charles Scribner's Sons, 1959.

6. Fromm, Erich *The Crisis of Psychoanalysis*. New York: Holt, Rinehart, and Winston, 1970.

7. Gordon, Thomas, M.D. *Pet in Action*. New York: Bantam Books, 1976.

8. Miller, Benjamin F., M.D. *The Complete Medical Guide*. New York: Simon and Schuster, 1956.

9. Montessori, Maria *The Absorbent Mind*. New York: Delta Books, 1967.

10. Ong, Beale H., M.D. *Doctor's Call Hour.* New York: Simon and Schuster, 1977.

11. Rogers, Carl R. *On Becoming a Person.* Boston: Houghton Mifflin Company, 1961.

12. Shawn, Ted *Every Little Movement.* New York: *Dance Horizons,* 1963.

13. Smith, Lendon H., M.D. *The Children's Doctor.* Englewood Cliffs, New Jersey: Prentice-Hall, 1969.

Index

52, 53, 83, 85, 86, 88, 90, 92,
93, 95, 96
Exercise materials, 6, 10, 16, 25,
26, 27, 28, 29, 30, 36, 38, 55,
59, 65-66, 69, 73, 74, 76, 77,
79, 97, 98, 101, 103, 109-10,
111, 113-14, 116-18, 120,
123, 124, 126, 128, 129, 131,
135, 137, 139
Exercise mats. *See* Blankets
and mats
Existential comprehension, by
child, 41
Expression, 83, 85
*Expressions of Emotion in Man
and Animals* (Darwin), 1
Extremities, 22, 26, 42, 57, 124

Face, 58
Fantasy, 90
Fast, concept of, 109, 110, 114
Fear, 21, 30, 47, 50, 92
Feet, 22, 27, 56-57
Flash cards, 74
Flexibility, 22, 27, 28, 33, 35
Flowers, 120, 121
Friends, participation in exer-
cises, 7, 38, 63, 64, 71, 74, 102
Fun, learning as, 52

Games, 51, 64, 68, 85, 89, 92,
101, 124
Ghosts, 133-34
Giving, concept of, 102
Globe, 128, 129, 131
"Good Morning," 25
Growing, 121
Guessing, 72
Guidance, 52, 84; self-, 88

"Hallowe'en," 133-34
Hamstrings, 26, 35
Hands, 57, 74
Harmonicas, 102
Head, 79

"Hear the Music," 37
Hips, 28, 31
"How do you do it?," 60
Humans, differences from other
life forms, 2-3, 22, 46

"I am a Piece of Clay," 69-71
Ice skating, 126, 127
Identity, 96
Illusion, 90
Imagination, 2, 90, 91, 93, 125
"I Make the Drum Talk," 101
"I Make the Music/I Make the
Dance," 102
Independence, 95
Index cards, 97
"Indian Dance, The," 135-36
Indians, 135
Individual, child as, 7, 96, 138
Indoors, 67
Infanthood, 83
Infantile sexuality, 43
Inside, concept of, 79
Integration, 85-87, 116, 120,
123, 125, 126, 128, 131, 133,
135, 139; definition, 85; of
abilities, 83; of abstract
thoughts, 5; of culture and
imagination, 91, 93; of physi-
cal and intellectual/social ex-
perience, 5-6, 22; through
movement, 84-85
Integration failures, 86
Intellectual functioning, 2
Intelligence, 90
Interaction, 63; of body parts, 55
Isabella, Queen, 131
"I Sit Up/I Lie Down," 29
Italy, 131

Knees, 57, 63, 68, 108

Language, 2, 8, 12, 23, 50, 88-89,
94, 95

Printed in the United States
122715LV00004B/149/A

9 780595 127016